The Last to Know

Published by Alderson Press
Nashville, Tennessee

ISBN: 978-0-578-01728-0

All of the characters in this book are fictitious, and any resemblance to actual persons, living or dead, is purely coincidental.

ACKNOWLEDGEMENTS

I would like to thank my sister, Betty Liddle, who was the first person to read the entire manuscript. She gave me feedback and encouragement.

Appreciation goes to fellow writers Pat Laster, Freeda Nichols, Rhonda Roberts and Winford Wallace. Among them, "seldom is heard a discouraging word." They helped me over some rough spots in the terrain of my storytelling, and Pat proved to be an astute copy editor.

Finally, special thanks to Steve May, my editor, for walking me through the final steps of putting a book together. His patience and expertise smoothed a harrowing road.

I also must mention my cheering squad, a host of family and friends, who root for me, support me and incite me to do my best.

Other titles by Dorothy Hatfield:

Every Day a New Day and Other Short Stories

"For I know the plans I have for you," declares the Lord,

"plans to prosper you and not to harm you,

plans to give you hope and a future."

Jeremiah 29:11

The Last to Know

Dorothy Hatfield

Chapter One

Sharon ran into the house and threw her things onto the kitchen counter. She grabbed the ringing phone.

"Is this the Timothy Jordan residence?"

"Yes."

"Is this Mrs. Jordan?"

"Yes." *Darn telemarketers.* She leaned across the counter and flipped through the mail.

"Mrs. Jordan, this is Lieutenant Roger Johnson of the Nebraska State Police. Your husband's been involved in an accident."

A letter dropped from her hand. "An accident? What happened?"

"A drunk driver hit your husband's car on Interstate 80 outside of Lincoln."

"Oh, my God! Is Tim hurt?" She stumbled to a chair, sat heavily.

"I'm sorry. Your husband was traveling east on I-80 and a car crossed the median ..."

"Wait a minute ... you said Interstate 80? You mean Lincoln, Nebraska?" She exhaled with relief. "I'm afraid there's some mistake. My husband's in Dallas."

Silence. "I see. Well, Mrs. Jordan ... um ... we made identification from the contents of a wallet ... ID belonging to Timothy Jordan of Burnsville, Arkansas. Will you verify your address?"

Hold it. How do I know this guy is a state trooper from Nebraska? He could be sitting at the end of the block talking on a cell phone. I've given him enough information.

"No. I can't help you." She clicked the receiver for a dial tone, punched the code for Tim's cell, missed a button and tried again.

"Hi, this is Tim. Leave a message after the beep."

"Tim, you can't believe the weird phone call I just got. Call me. Love you." She looked at her watch. *5:15 on Friday. His meeting should be over, but he might have plans for dinner. He'll call in a couple of minutes.*

She changed into jogging clothes, planning to run as soon as she heard from Tim. She began the warm-up exercises, slowly working out the kinks from sitting all day. Ten minutes passed.

Come on, Tim, call me. She gathered clothes from the hamper, walked to the utility room and loaded the washer. *His meeting must have run over. He'll call when he gets a chance. I'll eat first and jog later.*

Forty-five minutes later she dumped her half-eaten salad into the garbage and tried Tim again. She hung up on the voice mail message. *His phone probably needs charging. Maybe I'll call his hotel.*

He usually stayed at a Holiday Inn on I-635; she wasn't sure which one. She always called his cell if she needed him. By 6:30 pm, she knew that none of the Holiday Inns listed on Interstate 635 in Dallas had a Timothy Jordan registered.

She flipped through her address book, looking for an after-hours number for MetroComm. As Sales Representative for Corporate Accounts, Tim did much of his work at home through fax, telephone and computer, with occasional trips to Dallas or other cities to meet with clients.

Sharon and Tim loved the quiet life in Burnsville, near her folks and only 45 minutes from Little Rock. Often Sharon's workload at a graphic design studio in Woodbine allowed her to travel with Tim. In fact, she considered going along on this trip to Dallas, until Tim discouraged her, outlining a hectic schedule of meetings.

As she expected, the switchboard at MetroComm was closed. At random, she tried several people in the voice mail directory, finally leaving a message in the general mailbox.

Well, that was an exercise in frustration.

Her Christmas card list gave her Bill Sheridan's home address in Richardson, a suburb of Dallas, and Directory Assistance provided the number. Sharon sat at the kitchen table, looking at the telephone in her hand.

Okay, what do I do? Call my husband's boss, like some insecure wife, because two hours have gone by and he hasn't returned my call?

In her head, she rehearsed a lame excuse for calling, then punched in the number.

"This is the Sheridan residence. We can't come to the phone right…"

Sharon replaced the receiver. *Not going to leave a message. I'll call later. If I don't hear from Tim soon.* With a bottle of water from the fridge, she wandered into the living room, carrying the cordless phone.

The policeman from Nebraska … what was his name? … Jones? I should call him back. He said, '…involved in an accident,' didn't he? What if Tim actually did go to Lincoln for some reason? Or what if his billfold was lost or stolen? I could kick myself for not getting a phone number from Mr. Whatsisname.

She dialed the numbers Information gave her for the Nebraska State Police. *I'll find out if the guy who called is legit. What* was *his name?*

"I have no record of an officer name Jones or Jackson," the dispatcher told her.

"What about Johnson? I know it's a common name."

"There is a Lieutenant Roger Johnson in the traffic division. He went home at six."

"I understand. I just need some information about the accident."

"I'm sorry, Miss. I'm not at liberty to discuss any of our cases. Lt. Johnson is off until Monday, but he checks his messages regularly. Would you like his voice mail?"

She left a message for the officer to please call her regardless of the time.

Still holding the phone, she curled up in Tim's chair. *Why hasn't Tim called back? I need to talk to someone. Maybe Mother.* She dialed two digits and stopped. *Do I really want to tell Mother I don't know where Tim is? Besides, I need to leave the line open.*

Her thoughts vacillated between panic that her husband might be the injured man in Nebraska and confidence that Tim would walk through the door, having ended his meeting early, checked out of his hotel and come home. The explanation would be as simple as a malfunctioning cell phone and mistaken identity.

The doorbell broke the silence of the house. She scrambled out of the recliner, tripping on the afghan draped over her legs. *Tim's home. He forgot his key.* She yanked open the door. The man on the stoop looked vaguely familiar.

"Mrs. Jordan?" He opened his hand to display an official looking badge. "I'm John Wilson from the Sheriff's Department. May I come in?"

Her heart tightened. *Something really* has *happened to Tim.*

Chapter Two

On second look, she recognized Sheriff Wilson as a choir member at the First United Methodist Church, where she and Tim attended. Mr. Wilson opened a file folder and extracted a piece of paper.

"I'd like for you to look at this picture, please, and see if you know this man." He handed her a faxed copy of Tim's driver's license.

"That … that's my husband. Where did you get this?"

"Yes, I thought I recognized him, but I had to ask. I'm sorry, Mrs. Jordan, but according to the Nebraska state police, a man carrying this identification was killed instantly in a head on collision just outside of Lincoln."

"But my husband is in Dallas on business."

"Have you talked to him recently?"

"Well, no. I've left messages… Something must be wrong with his cell phone."

"Do you know why he might have been in Lincoln?"

"No. I told you, he left Tuesday on a business trip to Dallas. I don't expect him back until Sunday. He's attending a conference or something this weekend."

"Well, Mrs. Jordan, the Nebraska police have no reason to believe this is anything more than a traffic accident and your husband an innocent victim, but they would like for you to come to Lincoln to identify the body." Mr. Wilson shuffled the papers in his hands. "I'm deeply sorry. I met Tim last year at the Methodist Men's workday. He seemed like a good man. Can I call someone for you?"

He insisted on staying while she telephoned her parents. Earl and Sally Seabring owned a farm ten miles outside Burnsville. They would be at their daughter's home within half an hour.

Sharon hung up and turned to Mr. Wilson as he spoke into his cell phone, "I think we have a positive ID." Tears filled her eyes. *He's wrong. It can't be Tim.* She squeezed her lids shut and took a deep breath. Mr. Wilson closed his phone.

"My parents are on their way," she said. "I'll be fine. I'm sure you have other duties…"

"Certainly, Mrs. Jordan. I'll wait in my car until they come, if you don't mind."

"I'll be fine." She stood staring out the front window at the lights in the houses around the cul de sac. *Families watching TV together, putting children to bed. They don't know what's happened. They don't know Tim may be dead.* She wiped her face on her shirttail as Earl Seabring's pickup pulled into the drive.

Sharon's dad took his only child in his arms. "How you doing, Baby? You holding up?" Next, Sally held her for a long embrace. Sharon felt her mother's strength flow into her own wounded spirit.

"It's okay to cry, honey," Sally said, as she rocked Sharon in her arms.

"Yes, Mother. I just don't do that very well, you know."

They settled in the living room to talk for the next few hours. They discussed airline arrangements and Earl made the calls. Sharon didn't mention the questions about Tim's trip to Lincoln. He often traveled for MetroComm, so she let her parents assume he was in Nebraska on business when the accident happened. *I can't get my head around the fact that Tim must have lied to me about his trip to Dallas. I don't want to talk to anyone about it right now. Maybe later. When I find out the truth.*

Finally, Sally insisted Sharon try to sleep. In the bedroom she had shared with her husband, Sharon peeled off the jogging clothes and threw herself on the bed. She drew her knees up until she lay in a fetal position. Sobs wracked her body as the truth exposed all the denial that had held her together. Yesterday everything in her world seemed perfect. Now her husband was dead.

She slept fitfully, waking several times to throw her arm across Tim's side of the bed only to find it empty and think, *Oh, yes, he's in Dallas* – then immediately – *no, he's gone.*

At dawn, she left the bed and cupping her hands under the bathroom faucet, splashed her face. She stood at the open closet door. Looking in the mirror, Sharon considered her image, a tall strong body with a propensity for heavy thighs. *I can almost hear my biological clock ticking.*

They had not used birth control for three months. After years of college, Navy and career moves, Sharon and Tim wanted to start a family. One night, after a Christmas party at a neighbor's house, they walked home through the clear winter night. Sharon opened the subject.

"Do you ever think about having kids?"

"Us? Kids?"

"Yes, us. I'm not getting any younger, you know. We have a nice house. Both of us have good jobs. Insurance. A little money saved. It's time."

"It'll change our lives. Have you thought of that?"

"Sure. But, we're ready. I can't wait much longer. And I don't want to."

"Well, if you're sure..."

They had reached their front porch. Sharon turned and touched his face, her fingers tracing the line of his jaw. "I thought you loved kids."

"I do. Someone else's. Being responsible for another person scares me."

"We're grown up enough to do this." She tiptoed to kiss him. "You'll be a great daddy."

Jerking back to reality, Sharon shut the closet door. *No use thinking about that.* She dressed in jeans and shirt and slipped into the kitchen. Earl and Sally slept soundly in the guest room. Sharon took a cup of tea onto the deck and sat in the early morning sun.

Two squirrels ran across the back yard and up a budding tree. In another two weeks, the Bartlett Pear would be in bloom and the maple tree in the corner of the yard would be sending its little helicopter seeds all over the neighborhood. Sharon loved Arkansas, lush and green most of the year. She had gone to school in Oklahoma and had lived in several states during Tim's tour in the Navy. But, when the time came to buy a home, she couldn't wait to come back home.

Today's Saturday. Tim should be meeting friends for golf. She thought again of everything the deputy sheriff had said. *They want me to come to Lincoln.* She sipped the tea. *Maybe when I look, it won't be Tim.* She dreaded going back in the house. Before, when Tim was traveling, she had managed alone, but things were different now.

Where are you, Tim? Why aren't you here with me? Why were you in Nebraska? She buried her face in her hands. This time, she wept softly, for the loss deep inside her being.

I've spent hours sitting in church. Why didn't they teach me how to handle something like this? Losing someone I love. We were supposed to have a family – grandchildren – grow old together.

She'd heard people say they found comfort in prayer. To her, it sounded clichéd. *A canned response you give in Sunday School.* Praying was the last thing on her mind the afternoon before, when the police officer called. Or later, waiting to hear from Tim. *He was already dead by then. Praying wouldn't have changed that.*

Tim prayed every morning as he jogged through town. She knew this, even though they never discussed spiritual matters. He had tried a few times. "Have you ever thought about the meaning of life? Do you ever wonder why we're here?"

"Not unless I have to."

He had laughed, not forcing the conversation.

I don't like discussing my personal feelings. How I feel about God. But now, I wonder about life after death. I would love to believe Tim is alive somewhere. Her eyes filled. *What will I do without him?* She shook herself. *I need to get a grip. I need help.* She closed her eyes, causing tears to stream down her face. *God, can you help me get through this?*

Sharon sat very still, waiting for something to happen. A swoop of energy – a feeling – perhaps a revelation. She looked again at the calm scene in her yard. *I don't know if you heard me, God. But I promise one thing. Whether you help me or not, I won't rest until I discover the truth about Tim's death.*

***

Saturday passed. Sally took charge of answering the phone and doorbell as friends and neighbors heard the news. Mr. Wilson's wife must have alerted the United Methodist Women, because they immediately began bringing food and condolences. Earl busied himself with trips to the dry cleaner and other activities to help Sharon prepare for the trip to Lincoln – to bring Tim's body home.

Sharon's boss told her to take what time she needed. The small company officially provided five days bereavement leave, but they were always open to working with an employee during an emergency. Next she called Bill Sheridan at MetroComm in Dallas.

"I can't believe it," he said. "We had dinner together Thursday. The accident was in Lincoln, you say?"

"Yes." *So Bill didn't know about Tim's trip either.*

"I see." Bill paused politely. When she didn't comment, he went on, "Sharon, I'm so sorry. Tim was my friend. Just … well … let us know when the funeral plans are final."

Sharon replaced the receiver. She might need to talk to Bill about this later. *But not now, not just yet.* She sighed. Next she must call Bob Jordan, Tim's dad.

Tim had no siblings and in a short space of time, had virtually lost both his parents. After his mother died two years ago, it suddenly became clear that his dad was in the early stages of dementia. Without Mary, his wife of 40 years, to take care of him, to cover his mistakes and soothe his confusion, Bob's health declined rapidly. He still lived in Cedar, Texas, where Tim grew up, but no longer in their family home. An assisted living center with a part-time caregiver had proved to be the best solution. Sharon and Tim had placed his name on the waiting list of two long-term-care facilities in Arkansas. Someday he would need 24-hour care.

Maria, Bob's caregiver, answered his phone and Sharon gave her the gist of the message before talking to her father-in-law.

"Hello?"

"Hello, Bob. This is Sharon."

"Sharon?" The question in his voice indicated his confusion about who she might be.

"Yes. Sharon … you know … Tim's wife."

"Oh, yes. Tim's my son. Where is he?"

"Well, Bob, that's why I'm calling." Sharon paused. "There's been an accident."

"An accident? You tell Timmy he needs to be careful."

"I'm sorry. Tim's been hurt."

"Was he hurt real bad?"

"Yes. He … he's dead." She took a deep breath, stifled a sob.

"Dead?"

"Yes. Bob? Are you all right?"

"I'm okay. But I don't think we should tell his mother. It would make her too sad."

"His mother? Oh. Bob…?

"Well, I gotta go. It's fixing to rain. You tell Timmy to be careful. His mother doesn't like for him to get hurt."

Maria came back on the line. She agreed with Sharon that it would be best if Bob didn't attend the funeral. No point in confusing him further. Sharon gave Earl the names of two cousins and an aunt to notify. He would call them later. Plans for the service couldn't be finalized until after Sharon returned. Her flight left the next afternoon, Sunday. It took all the grit she could muster to keep up a show of emotional strength and to convince her parents she could make the trip alone.

She had no idea what she might find in Lincoln.

Chapter Three

"Mrs. Jordan? Hello. I'm Roger Johnson." The tall police lieutenant extended his hand as Sharon walked into the reception area of the State Crime Laboratory building in Lincoln on Monday morning. She nodded a greeting and he continued. "I want to apologize for the telephone call the night of your husband's accident. I should have waited until we had completed the identification."

When Sharon didn't respond, he asked, "How was your flight?"

"Fine. When can I see my husband?"

"Well … okay … why don't we go to my office."

She followed him down a hall and sat on the edge of the chair he indicated.

"Now, Mrs. Jordan, did you bring anyone with you?"

"No, I made the trip alone. Why?"

"Well, we need for you to officially identify the body and that may be … uh … difficult for you. It would be good if you weren't alone."

"I am fine. I just want to see my husband."

"Okay. Now, this is going to be different from viewing someone at a funeral, you know. Are you sure…?"

"I. Am. Fine." Lips tight and jaw clinched.

Without speaking further, he escorted her to the basement floor and through the maze of halls to the morgue. As she stepped through the swinging doors, she shivered. The temperature had to be no more than 40 degrees. A strange odor invaded her nostrils. The lieutenant signed the log and they entered the vault area. An attendant pulled out drawer #356 and lifted the linen sheet from the face of the body lying on the slab. Despite her resolve, Sharon gasped and stepped back. The bruised and distorted face did indeed belong to Timothy Jordan. No doubt about it; her husband was dead.

Back in Johnson's office, she gratefully accepted the cup of coffee. The hot liquid slid down her throat, the caffeine calmed her nerves.

"Excuse me, Mrs. Jordan, I'll be back in a few minutes."

As soon as the door shut behind him, Sharon grabbed a handful of tissues off the desk and buried her face in their white softness, sobbing. When the officer returned, she had regained her composure, her puffy eyes and red nose the only evidence of what had taken place in his absence.

"Mrs. Jordan, I'm so sorry for your loss. I have been at this job twenty years but this is one phase where I've never gained much expertise."

She inhaled deeply and held it for a moment before breathing out. *Well, I'm sure not going to make it easier for you.*

"The next thing we need for you to do is sign the papers agreeing to the autopsy."

"Autopsy?"

"Yes. It's routine. We have no reason to believe Mr. Jordan was mixed up in anything shady, but since he was here under unusual circumstances, we would like to investigate further."

"No one mentioned an autopsy."

"No, I guess not. I'm sorry." He moved some papers on his desk.

"I have a feeling you can proceed without my signature."

"Yes, we could. It would just take a little longer." He cleared his throat. "Do you have any idea why your husband might have been in Nebraska?" *This is why they're suspicious. He died in Lincoln when his wife thought he was in Dallas.*

"No. Business of some sort, I'm sure." She sat up straighter.

"Had you noticed anything unusual about your husband lately? Maybe, behavior that seemed strange?"

"Of course not. Nothing." *Only that he's been distracted and preoccupied for the past several weeks. Often so lost in thought he seemed to forget I existed.*

Lt. Johnson laid a sheaf of papers and a pen on the desk. When she finished signing, he said, "The autopsy will take about three days. Where will we be able to reach you?"

"What?"

"Where will you be staying? I asked Pathology to put a rush on it, but the body won't be released until Wednesday at the earliest."

"What am I supposed to do until Wednesday?" Sharon made no effort to be polite.

"I'm sorry, Mrs. Jordan." The Lieutenant looked as though he would give half his pension to be anywhere else in the world at that moment.

Sharon gave him the number of her hotel and left the police building, grateful to be in the fresh air. Since she would be staying over, she was glad she hadn't checked out of her room. She could keep the rental car and change the return date on her flight with a couple of phone calls. On an impulse, and with some directions from Roger Johnson, she drove out Interstate 80, away from the city.

She knew what she looked for but didn't know it would be so easy to spot. As she passed the numbered mile marker Lt. Johnson had given her, she saw a white cross decorated with flowers and streamers. Carefully pulling onto the shoulder, she stopped the car. She walked through the chewed-up grass and stepped over the gouged earth. A satin ribbon, emblazoned with three Greek letters, a college fraternity symbol, lay beneath the cross. Another, attached to a bouquet, declared, "Jason, we will miss you."

Sharon fell to her knees and wept. After a time, she stood and said, "Tim, *I* will miss *you*."

She drove back to the city. She had not eaten since breakfast at the hotel, so she went to a drive-through and bought a hamburger and fries. *Okay. So my legs get fat. The heck with it.* In her hotel room that evening, she recalled the police officer's question, "Have you noticed anything unusual about your husband's behavior?" She didn't admit to him that Tim had been acting strangely for several weeks. Now that she thought about it, she was sure that something was bothering him. She tried to think of a reason for this secret trip. *If I were a detective in the movies or TV, I could use this time to follow up on clues. If I had a clue.*

She didn't know a soul in Lincoln. And neither did Tim, so far as she knew. What was he doing here? Where would that information be? *In his notebook. Or in his computer.*

Tim lived by his notebook. When he made an appointment, he entered it immediately. His destination in Lincoln would be in his daily planner.

Excited at the break-through, she jumped out of her chair and twirled around. *Of course! He keeps his notebook in his briefcase.* She sat down, deflated. *Which is with his luggage. And the police must have everything from inside the car.* She hadn't thought to ask Johnson about Tim's personal possessions.

She paced the small room. She could do nothing about any of this until she returned to Burnsville and found some private time to look through Tim's belongings and search his computer. Until then... *Let the police investigate. They have the equipment and manpower. I'll wait. When they release his body, they should release his luggage, too.*

She spent the next two days walking the malls, talking on the phone to her boss, taking care of what business she could (*why didn't I bring my laptop?*) and keeping her parents up to date. This delay required a whole new set of lies to them. She would explain later, when she felt like talking about it.

On Wednesday afternoon, Sharon signed the receipt and a uniformed officer put Tim's bags into the car. Lt. Johnson told her the preliminary report on the autopsy showed nothing significant. The police had discovered Tim flew from Dallas to Lincoln on Friday morning and rented a car at the airport. He was traveling south on I-80 when a 19-year-old college student lost control of his automobile, crossed the median and hit the rental car head-on. Both drivers died at the scene. Alcohol and drugs were found in the younger man's car.

Tim's body was loaded in the cargo hold of the plane for the trip home, Sharon's questions still unanswered, Tim's death still a mystery.

Chapter Four

Sharon fought the familiar sinking feeling as the airplane's wheels left the ground. She had never become accustomed to the scary sensation during lift off. She – and Tim – would land in Little Rock at dinnertime. Tim's funeral was set for Saturday in Burnsville. Mercifully, the process had moved along easily. *I'm ready for something to be easy.*

On Roger Johnson's suggestion, she contacted a mortician in Lincoln, who picked up Tim's body at the morgue and made all the necessary arrangements for the funeral home in Burnsville to meet the plane. Sharon could contact them later for the final details. She would meet with Reverend Jerry Thompson of First United Methodist Church tomorrow morning to plan the service. For this moment, there was nothing to do. She lay her head against the seat back and thought of happier times. Of how it began…

***

Sharon Seabring met Tim Jordan while he served at the Naval Station in Norman, Oklahoma and she was a freshman at O.U. One night, her roommate took her to a party out at someone's rambling ranch house that sat on fifteen acres of flat pastureland. Most of the guests were strangers to Sharon, being members of the college/career class her roommate attended at New Life Church in downtown Norman. The crowd was congenial and fun. It was game night and noisy groups gathered playing table games or charades. More than an hour passed before Sharon noticed a young man sitting alone observing the activity around him. She watched him discreetly for awhile, trying to decide if he was with someone. Finally, she walked over and sat in a chair across from him.

"What's a nice boy like you doing in a place like this?" He looked up and gave her the most amazing smile she had ever seen. *Wow!* "Hi, I'm Sharon."

They fell into an easy conversation and spent the rest of the evening talking. As they exhausted one topic, Sharon opened another with a cliché pick up line: "What's your sign?" or "Read any good books lately?" Tim laughed easily and went along with the gag. By the end of the evening, they had plans for lunch the next day.

At Thanksgiving break, Sharon visited Tim's parents in Texas. They spent Christmas together at the Seabring's farm in Arkansas. By the end of the spring semester, they were engaged. Shortly after he returned from the Persian Gulf, they took their wedding vows before the altar in the little country church where Sharon attended Vacation Bible School. Tim left the Navy as soon as his hitch was up. They were eager to settle down.

And settle they did, into the routine of small town life: a new house, advancing careers, golf on Saturday, church on Sunday and regular family gatherings. Time flew by.

***

Sharon looked out the airplane window at the tops of the clouds over northwest Arkansas. She thought again of the evening she opened the conversation about babies, smiling as she remembered their last New Year's Eve together. She had been so excited at the prospect of starting a family. And Tim had been…

She sat up straight in her seat. Tim had been – well – almost diffident. *And that was when it started. His preoccupation. The times when he was suddenly lost in thought, hardly aware of my presence. I don't get it. We were always pretty open with each other. I would have staked my life on his loyalty. And I believe he trusted me completely. Why would he be reluctant to bring a child into this family? If he didn't want children, why didn't he just say so?*

The tires of the jet squealed on the runway. Sharon gathered her carry-on bag and moved into the aisle.

I love you, Tim. I've never invaded your privacy. I don't know what it is you couldn't tell me, but I'll find out somehow. I must know the truth.

Chapter Five

"Mother, I'm meeting Reverend Thompson at ten. Will you come along?" Sharon and Sally sat on the deck, drinking coffee. Sally had packed a bag, come to Burnsville and spent every night since Tim died. Sharon usually rejected her mother's hovering presence, but since she had no clue about making funeral arrangements or planning a memorial service, she needed help. Sally was happy to oblige.

"I'm so sorry to hear about Tim's accident," the pastor said, as they settled in his office. "He and I were close friends. I could talk to him in confidence, bounce ideas or concerns off him. It was … good to know him." He blinked rapidly and paused before he continued. "If you don't mind, I'd like to include some personal remembrances of Tim."

"Of course. That would be … nice." *What a surprise. I had no idea that Tim and this man were any more than casual acquaintances.*

"Do you have a favorite scripture? Or maybe one of Tim's?"

"Why don't you choose something … or, oh … I guess the 23rd Psalm…"

"All right. And something from the New Testament? Is there anything particular you would like me to say, that you would like people to know about Tim. Or be reminded of?"

Sharon thought of the questions surrounding Tim's death, of the doubts that flooded her mind. "Yes," she said. "He was a good man."

***

"There may not be a visitation," Sharon said to Sally as they left the church. "I'm not sure I can stand there for two hours and let people tell me how sorry they are for me. It's so maudlin."

"Well ... dear..." Sally seemed to be choosing her words carefully. "I think you'll be sorry later if you don't do this."

"Why? I don't want to see anyone. All I want is to be left alone. I can't seem to stop crying and I hate that."

"It's okay to cry. It's normal. You don't have to be so stoic. It's okay for others to see you cry. I'll bet Tim had a lot of friends in this church. A visitation is as much for them as for you. So they can pay their last respects."

"Why do I have to think about what they need or want? I'm the one who lost a husband."

"Sharon, you're tired." Sally reverted to the excuse she always used when Sharon misbehaved as a child. They reached the car and Sally opened the door and sat in the passenger seat before she spoke again. "Honey, you're not alone. You're not the only one who lost Tim. Your daddy and I loved him like a son." She fished in her jacket pocket for a handkerchief, turned her head toward the window, reached under her glasses to dab at her eyes.

In the end, Sharon bowed to all the southern traditions: receiving friends at Baxter and Sons Funeral Home on Friday evening, services in the church sanctuary on Saturday afternoon with lunch provided by the United Methodist Women beforehand, burial in Burnsville Cemetery out on Highway 5.

At 5:30 on Friday, Sally tapped on the bedroom door. The two women had spent the morning choosing pictures for a video. Sharon pulled out Tim's Point of Grace CD for pre-service music and delivered it to the church. Unexpectedly, she found comfort in looking at pictures of their life together and listening to Tim's favorite songs. After lunch, physically and emotionally drained, she went to her room to rest.

"Are you ready, Honey? Your Daddy is..." Sally stopped at the sight of Sharon's bed piled high with discarded clothes.

"Mother, I have no idea what to wear to this thing tonight. What's the proper attire for a wake, anyway?" Sharon's voice broke and she sank to the floor, surrounded by shoes.

"Come on now. You've been to visitations before. Just wear anything comfortable. Do you want me to help you choose?" A smile played around Sally's mouth. "That would probably help you decide. When you were little, I'd suggest something and you'd pick the opposite." She went to the open closet door. "See, here's some perfectly lovely sweats. Shall I find your Reeboks?"

"Oh, Mother, please." Sharon rose, rummaged through the thrown-off clothes and located grey slacks and white silk blouse. "Let's get this over with."

Later, reflecting on the evening, Sharon thought she must have stood the entire two hours with her mouth agape, as one person after another told her how Tim had touched their lives.

"Your husband was such a kind man. He gave me a lift to the doctor nearly every week."

"Tim came by and helped us move. Couldn't have done it without him."

"...such a loving man." "...so caring." "...so generous." "...a true Christian."

Where did these people come from? They all seem to know Tim. Where was I when this was going on? She glanced at her watch. *Ten more minutes. I can stand ten more minutes. But, they're still coming in the door.*

"Excuse me."

She had seen the teenager come in and sit near the entrance.

"My ... my name is Eric. I just wanted to tell you..." He paused, tears forming in his eyes. He cleared his throat. "I just want you to know what a great guy Tim was. Well, I guess you know that, but he was so cool. There just never will be another like him. I miss him so much already."

"You knew Tim? Where?"

"Well, I thought maybe he would've told you. Last year, I was so messed up … in Juvenile Hall. My parents had about given up on me. Anyway, Brother Thompson asked Tim if he would take me on … like help me get straightened out."

"Really? Like a mentor?"

"I guess. I was pretty bummed at the whole idea, but Tim took me to Little Rock to a Travelers' game, then to a pizza place. We were sitting there, all having fun and everything and he gave me a good talking to. Like, did I want to end up in prison? He put me on a program for school and homework. Then, later, he sat down with my parents and me and helped us talk to each other. Anyway, he was such a great guy. I'm sure you know that, being married to him and all. I said thanks to him and everything, but I just wanted you to know."

The boy rubbed his hand on his jeans then extended it toward Sharon. She squeezed it in return, wracking her brain to fit what he was saying into her memory. *I remember Tim going to a baseball game occasionally. With the guys, he said. He worked at home a lot, and he obviously took time out to help with projects at the church. Besides all the good things I know about, there seems to be twice as many that happened in secret. Mother was right. It's not just my loss, but the world's. Oh Tim, you were such a loving man. I just can't understand it. Why did you lie?*

CHAPTER SIX

The door to the small bedroom, converted into Tim's workspace, had been closed since the Tuesday morning he left for Dallas. A week and a day had passed since that first phone call from Roger Johnson. During that time, Sharon had hardly a moment alone to grieve or to process all that had happened. The funeral service over, her parents gone back to their own home, Sharon's opportunity to investigate Tim's belongings had finally come.

She lay the briefcase retrieved from the Nebraska police on the desk and flipped on the power supply to the computer. Opening the case, she took out Tim's notebook, where he kept his business appointments and personal information. Maybe he had made a note that would tell her something. *Too easy, too good to be true, to find the answer written out for me.*

She turned the calendar pages randomly, reluctant to look at Tuesday, March 9, the day Tim left for Dallas. Seeing his familiar, impatient scribble on each page, her breath caught in her throat. Her finger traced the broad pen strokes as the reality of his death descended on her again. At the top of each page was written ***JWG.*** The first time she saw this, Sharon asked Tim what the initials stood for.

"Jog With God. I put the most important things on my schedule first." And he had grinned and punched her playfully on the arm. His faithfulness impressed her. She stared at the letters. *Whatever it was Tim had going with God, I wish I had some of it in my life.*

Tuesday, March 9, 2004

12:00 noon ***Meet with Bill***

Meet with Bill. So, he did have a meeting at MetroComm on Tuesday. Wednesday and Thursday were filled with details of various MetroComm appointments. Clearly, he had been in Dallas. Then…

Friday, March 12, 2004

8:00 a.m. ***Flight 972***

1:00 p.m. ***Newton, NE***

7:00 p.m. ***Flight 363 to DFW***

Call Sharon

Newton? Is that a town in Nebraska? I never heard of it, but that doesn't mean much. The first time I set foot in Nebraska was last Sunday.

Pulling out the atlas, she soon found the town of Newton, fifty or sixty miles from Lincoln, population 2400. And I-80 would be the logical route.

That's where Tim was headed when he was killed. Keep an appointment there at 1:00 and catch a plane back to Dallas that night. And he was going to call me. To tell me what?

Most of the customers Tim dealt with worked for large corporations; his trips were always to major cities. Sharon couldn't think of an occasion when he called on a customer in a small town. The trip to Nebraska had to be personal business.

What personal business could he have that I wouldn't know about? And which of the two thousand people in Newton, Nebraska did Tim plan to see? Maybe there's something in his email.

She knew his password: 61291 – their anniversary.

As she scanned his inbox, a message from **biggirlnow** caught her attention. It was sent on the day Tim died. Sharon clicked the cursor to open the mail.

Date: March 12, 2004

From: biggirlnow

To: tjordan

I'm so sorry you didn't come. I was looking forward to seeing you. Did you tell your wife? Did things go bad? Now that we found each other I don't want to lose you.
Love, "Hannah"

Sharon stared at the screen. *So this is it. The wife is always the last to know. And he was going to tell me?* Through a blur, she read the other messages on the screen, but found nothing significant, nothing that would give her information about the strange note from Hannah.

Returning to the planner, she saw a yellow sticky note protruding from the address pages. She pulled it loose.

3/12/04

1:00 p/u Eve

Bens

2500 Tab—

Sharon read the note several times. *Who is Eve? Did Tim have* two *other women in his life? The letters p/u might be shorthand for 'pick up.' Pick up Eve. At one o'clock. So that was the appointment in Newton. 'Tab' could be an abbreviation also. Tablets, maybe? And Bens? What does that mean?*

Sharon gasped. Her hand flew to her mouth. *Bens. Ecstasy!* She knew very little about illegal drugs but she watched television enough to know that 'bens' was a street name for ecstasy. *And Eve – another name for Ecstasy! Tim was going to meet with someone in Nebraska and pick up 2500 tablets of Ecstasy!*

Sharon walked quickly out of the office, as though by leaving that room she could escape this evidence she had uncovered. She crossed the den and stood at her patio door watching the birds gather at the feeder. The buds on the dogwood, encouraged by the warm weather, were ready to break into blooms. She longed to remain there and concentrate on the beauty in her back yard rather than face the truth she had been determined to find. Tim – mixed up in drug trafficking. No matter how much she wanted to deny it, she couldn't. The more she thought about it the more she knew, in her heart, it was the only scenario that made sense.

This is contrary to everything Tim professed belief in. And, how on earth could he hope to get away with it? How did he plan to get past all the security in the airports nowadays? Let's see, 2500 tablets would fit into twenty-five prescription bottles. It could be hidden in his luggage.

The Nebraska police had obviously not found any such thing in the car or they would still be investigating. Tim must have been on his way to pick up the drugs when the accident happened.

And where does Hannah fit into all this? Is she his contact? Sharon looked around for something to break. Her rage was suddenly so uncontrollable that she felt only a drastic action would release it. She now understood why a man might put his fist through a wall, a phenomena that had completely eluded her before today. Finding nothing she wanted to destroy, or clean up, she said aloud, "Okay, you said you'd get at the truth. Now keep going."

A tab in the back of the notebook read 'JWG Prayers.' Sharon flipped over and read a list of names jotted randomly followed by what was obviously a concern: health, job, grief, etc. On the second page of these notes she saw her own name. "Sharon needs a nudge. Should I? Or remain a quiet witness? She's so close and yet so far."

What did he mean by that? Is he talking about me? Close to what? Never mind. I can't deal with any more mystery right now.

She slowly turned backward through the date-book pages, reading. She saw lunch dates, a dental appointment, a reminder to call his dad on his birthday, meetings with Eric – all items that detailed the life of her husband. A man she wondered if she knew at all.

A tear dropped on the page where her hand rested. January 15. Tim had written something along the margin. She blinked and looked closer. The words 'Joy Ann' and a ten-digit phone number. She recognized the area code for East Texas. *Another woman? This is too much.* She grabbed the phone and punched the keypad furiously.

"Hello."

"Hello … uh … my name is Sharon Jordan." She had not thought of what she might say when someone answered. "I'm Tim Jordan's wife. May I ask who I'm talking to?"

"This is Joy Ann Bullard."

"Well," Sharon said steadily, "I found your number in my dead husband's book."

"T-Tim is dead?" The voice on the other end of the line wavered.

"You knew my husband?"

"A long time ago. What happened?"

"I was hoping *you* could tell *me*." Sharon did not try to disguise her bitterness.

"Yes, I suppose we need to talk. But I'd rather it be face to face. Is that possible?"

The Public Library in Texarkana was chosen as a halfway mark. *And neutral ground. And safe, in case Joy Ann Bullard turns out to be part of a drug ring.*

The next day, Sharon spent the two-hour drive to the Arkansas-Texas border town trying to collect her thoughts and prepare to meet a woman who had some sort of place in Tim's life. Would this Joy Ann be able to tell her about Hannah? Would she be willing to reveal what she knew about Tim's involvement with illegal drugs? Sharon could only hope for answers.

Chapter Seven

In spite of her resolve to hate Joy Ann Bullard, Sharon was impressed by the composure of the attractive woman sitting across the table in the small cubicle. *She doesn't look like the 'other woman.' And she probably isn't. Hannah is.*

Sharon spoke first. She told Joy Ann only about the automobile accident, holding back any mention of drug deals and ending with, "I just need some answers. Who are you? How do you know my husband? And can you tell me why he was in Nebraska?"

"Tim found me in January through a classmate website. We were high school … well … sweethearts." She looked away from Sharon, focusing on the surface of the table. "In our junior year, I got pregnant. I wondered if he had ever mentioned me to you."

"Oh. No, I … I didn't know."

"When they found out, our parents had a fit. They made all our decisions for us. Maybe they had to. We were entirely too young. They sent me to a place in San Antonio. I gave up the baby for adoption."

Tim never told me!

"I guess it was the best thing," Joy Ann continued. "Afterward, I lived with an aunt in North Carolina. I finished school there. Our folks wouldn't let us see each other. Tim never knew where I was. Later I heard he had joined the Navy. A couple of times I thought about trying to find him, but I didn't know where to start."

"Then, he found you … two months ago."

"Yes. He was really looking for Hannah."

"Hannah?"

"Our daughter."

"Your daughter?" Sharon heard herself echoing everything Joy Ann said.

"Tim said you two were trying to start a family. He admitted he hadn't thought much about our child through the years, but now he was wondering what had happened to our baby. His first child that he had never known. He said he had thought a lot about it and decided he wanted to find her. He didn't tell you?"

"No." *But he thought a lot about it.*

"Texas has open adoption. I knew the name of her adoptive parents and could have been involved in her life to whatever extent we agreed on. After they moved up north I didn't see her very often, but I always knew how to contact her."

"So, Hannah is your daughter."

"Yes. Well, Hannah is the name I gave her. I've always called her that, at least in my head. They named her Eve."

Eve! Sharon took a deep breath. "And you told Tim how to find her?"

"Yes. She's a young woman now. Her last name is Bens and she lives in Newton, Nebraska. I assume that's where he was going."

"And her address…"

"I don't remember exactly. Tableau Avenue, I think."

"2500 Tab…leau."

"Maybe. I'd have to check."

***

Sharon pulled off State Street onto the I-30 ramp, headed back to Burnsville. She had said goodbye to Joy Ann Bullard almost reluctantly, feeling there were more questions to be answered. But still wondering who might have the truth.

Tim has a daughter. He obviously tried to forget about her. All these years... And he never told me... Then he changed his mind ...wanted to meet her ... but before he can ... She felt the sting of tears behind her eyes. *Wow! For someone who hates to cry, lately I boo-hoo at the drop of a hat.* She pounded her fist on the steering wheel. *I want to see her. I want to meet Tim's daughter.*

One week later, Sharon sat in a plane on the tarmac at Little Rock Airport, the steady hum and vibration of the jet engines adding to the anticipation she felt. The email and phone calls to Eve had resulted in an invitation to the Bens home in Newton, Nebraska.

When she explained the situation to her parents, the conversation with Sally and Earl had gone well. They loved Tim. They would have supported his decision to find his daughter. Bob Jordan would never know his grandchild. Lost in his dementia, he had not yet grasped the fact of Tim's death.

The engines revved and the familiar knot formed in her stomach. *I'm really in uncharted waters, meeting Tim's child. I don't know if I can stand it.*

The light flashed and she fastened her seat belt as the pilot's voice came over the intercom, "Welcome to Flight 1525. It's a sunny 70 degrees in Lincoln and it should be a beautiful trip, so sit back and relax."

The runway whizzed past. Tomorrow, she would complete Tim's journey. And begin a pilgrimage of her own.

Chapter Eight

"Mrs. Jordan? I thought that was you."

Sharon recognized the voice. In the micro-second before she turned from the display of maps to acknowledge the greeting, she wondered if there was some place to run to avoid seeing the man again. After renting the car at the Lincoln airport, she stopped at a Visitor's Center to kill some time and get her bearings. She never expected to see anyone she knew.

"Hello, Lt. Johnson." Her voice was polite but devoid of any warmth.

"I'm surprised to see you. I assumed you would never want to set foot in Nebraska again."

"You're not far from wrong. But sometimes things happen to change one's mind."

"I see."

Silence. Finally Roger Johnson continued. "I notice ... er ... are you looking for a map? If I can give you any assistance, please, allow me..."

Bumpkin! With those people skills, how in the world did you get your job? To her surprise, Sharon felt a tinge of empathy.

"Actually, I probably don't need a map. I'm driving to Newton. I understand there's an exit off I-80."

"Newton? Yes, take Exit 123, I think it is. Anyway, State Highway 59. Newton is about 25 miles. It's a little town, two or three thousand or so."

She knew he was curious but ignored it. *I have no idea what this trip to see Eve will require of me. I surely don't want to discuss it with a stranger, even one trying to be helpful.* She returned the map to the rack with finality.

The officer spoke again. "I have thought..." He cleared his throat. "I wondered how you managed the trip back to Arkansas. It must have been hard."

"I did fine. I had ... help."

"Good, good. Look, I just stopped here for lunch. Would you like something to eat, or a cup of coffee, or something?"

"No, thank you, I don't think so."

"Mrs. Jordan ... Sharon ... I'm sure that just to look at me brings up a lot of bad memories for you. But you can't imagine how much I would like to be of help. Please give me a chance to be a friend." He handed her a business card. "Will you promise to call me if you need anything while you're here? Or, maybe you'll want to talk to someone after your trip to Newton..."

Sharon raised her head quickly and met his gaze. *Why would he say that? What did he know? He's probably just guessing that whatever made me fly from Arkansas to a tiny town in nowhere Nebraska must be involved and heavy. I'm just jumpy. I guess I could use a break.*

"Okay, maybe a glass of tea. But let's talk about the weather."

Thirty minutes later, Sharon and Roger parted, having moved to a first-name basis. She had learned that the dogwood is the state tree of Nebraska just as it is Arkansas, and he received a short geology lesson about the caves and mineral springs throughout the Natural State.

Standing beside her rental car, Sharon offered him her hand. "Thank you for a pleasant break. I'm sorry if I seemed aloof earlier. I ... I'm still kinda raw."

"I know." He extracted another card from his shirt pocket, turned it over and wrote a number on the back. "This is my cell. Please call if you need anything. We want the visitors to our state to have an enjoyable stay."

Sharon pulled onto the highway, smiling at the encounter. *I guess I'll have to admit he's a nice man. I sure didn't think so the first time we met. But, he tries to be helpful. He's just such a dork! Bumbling and fumbling every thing he says. Except ... when he said 'I know' just now, it sounded like maybe he really did.*

Her attention snapped sharply back to the present as she passed the white cross alongside the road. The original bouquets had been replaced and the flowers drooped in the warm spring sunshine. Sharon felt a surge of anger at the college boy who, stoned out of his head, killed her husband. She seethed with irritation at his friends who built this shrine to someone who would act so irresponsibly. *What about Tim? He'll never be the great daddy he would have been, or the doting grandpa. All because of some little twerp named Jason.*

She thought back to a conversation with Reverend Thompson while planning Tim's memorial service. She expressed her bitterness and anger to the minister, thinking he might say something to help her get a grip on what had happened to her life.

"You know, you will never find peace until you can forgive this young man," he had said. "His parents are hurting just as you are. They lost a son. His death is just as tragic to them as Tim's is for you."

This comment made her furious and it took all the acumen she had to not lash out at the pastor. Instead she had changed the subject back to the task at hand. *I'll have to give the man credit, he was very helpful with plans for the service. Tim's memorial was a true celebration of his life.*

Tears blurred Sharon's vision and she almost missed the Newton exit. *I can't do this. I need to focus.* She punched buttons until she found an Oldies station with 'hits from the 80s and beyond.'

Highway 59 became Main Street in Newton. She drove through the attractive downtown area and turned right on Tableau. Pulling up in front of number 2500, she sat for a minute, her fingers gripping the steering wheel. *Too late for cold feet. Eve is expecting you. Go do what you can for this girl who lost the dad she never had a chance to know.*

Sharon rang the bell and heard movement inside. The young woman who opened the door extended her hand. "Hi, you're Sharon, aren't you? I'm so glad you came. I'm Eve Bens."

Sharon took the proffered hand and hoped her face did not reflect her surprise. No one had mentioned that Eve was in a wheelchair.

Chapter Nine

"Come on in. I can tell by the look on your face that Joy Ann didn't tell you I had wheels."

Sharon stepped inside, unable to think of a reply. Eve continued to speak as she rolled across the entryway and into the living room.

"Now that I think about it, it wasn't very nice of me not to tell you myself. I guess I wanted to be sure this visit wasn't a pity party. But it was rude. Forgive me?"

Sharon shrugged. "I suppose I understand. We've all been dealing with a lot of new things. I've been operating on raw emotion myself. Do you … uh … want to tell me … what happened?"

"To put me in this chair? A swimming accident, two weeks after I graduated from high school. So much for all the 'your future is ahead of you' commencement speeches."

"I'm sorry."

"I'm managing. Actually, most of the time I'm doing great. Sit down. Would you like something to drink?"

Sharon settled into an overstuffed chair across from Eve. "Not right now, thanks. Do you want to talk about Tim?"

"Sure. He and I never met face to face. We talked on the phone and emailed several times. I'm so … crushed that I never got to know him."

"He was a wonderful man. He never told … he didn't get a chance to tell me about you."

"He didn't get a chance? How long were you married?"

"Okay, you're right. I think he wanted to meet you himself first."

"Yeah. So you've got to have some kind of feelings about that."

"Yes. Uh … Eve … maybe I will take some water."

"Sure." The younger woman spun the chair and wheeled out of the room. Sharon took a moment to look around. A spinet covered with family photographs. A studio portrait of a child above the fireplace. An entertainment center and a bookcase, filled with medical dictionaries and best selling novels.

Sharon rose for a closer look at the picture above the mantel. The child sat on a stool, her white dress spread to show lace trim. Soft curls fell around her shoulders. Tim's eyes stared from under the short cropped bangs.

"Cute, huh? My first communion." Eve re-entered the room balancing a tray expertly on the arms of her chair while negotiating the wheels. "I brought cookies, too."

"It's a precious picture. You were about six?"

"Yes. My mother loves it. Reminds her of easier times, I guess."

"I can't imagine how it must hurt to see a child face difficulty. We never … I never had any children."

"Do you mind … will you tell me about my dad?"

"Of course, that's what I came for."

The next hours sped by as Eve learned about her biological father. Sharon wanted Eve to know the strong personality, deep faith, loyalty and commitment that were so much a part of Tim. From time to time, Eve asked questions, wanting to know more, and Sharon tried to be honest. When the conversation wound down, a box of tissues sat empty, witness to the released emotion in the room.

Sharon drew a long drink from the bottle of Evian before she spoke again. "If you're up to it, I would really like to know more about you. We've shared a loss. I feel like there's a bond between us."

"Sure. My life was pretty normal for the first eighteen years. My parents explained adoption to me as soon as I was old enough to understand. Joy Ann sent me cards and came to see me once in a while. I never knew about Tim until recently."

"Weren't you curious?"

"I was a happy kid without much curiosity. But, on my fifteenth birthday, Joy Ann was visiting and I asked her about my birth dad. She told me his name, but said she'd lost track of him. I figured when I got older I'd try to look him up. Then ... well ... my life got complicated."

"What about that? I don't want to pry..."

"It's okay. I was swimming at the lake with a bunch of friends and the water wasn't as deep as I thought. I hit my head on the bottom and the impact damaged my spinal cord. I'm paralyzed from the waist down. An inch higher and I would have lost use of my hands, a few more inches up and I would have needed assistance breathing. Like Superman. You know, Christopher Reeve."

Eve gave the chair a little turn. "Mom and Dad wanted me to have a motorized chair, so I have one for getting around school. But my physical therapist says since I *can* use my upper body I should push this one for the exercise. Unused muscles atrophy." She turned to face Sharon and continued. "For a long time I wondered why this happened to me. Then, as I realized how much worse it could be, I wondered why I had been so lucky. Like ... why had God protected me from the extreme injury others have suffered in the same kind of accident? What am I supposed to do with my life now?"

"I don't understand. You think God kept you from being totally paralyzed for a reason?"

"Yes, I do. And I think he let me almost meet Tim for a reason. That's the only way I can bear the fact that we came so close and still missed each other. It all has to be a part of God's plan. I just have to figure out what I'm supposed to do with it."

"Do you think God wanted Tim to die for a reason?"

"That's a hard question. I haven't figured out if God plans all these things … you know, like predestination … or if he takes all the stuff that happens to us and makes something good out of it, if we let him."

"That's an interesting viewpoint. I've been blaming the drunk kid."

"Well, me too, some. Seems like we need *someone* to be responsible for the bad things. After my accident, I blamed myself for not checking the depth of the water I dove into. And I spent some time thinking the other kids should have stopped me. But let's face it, teenagers do dumb things. Sometimes people get hurt."

"You're very mature for your age."

Eve laughed. "Only recently. If you've got time, I'll tell you about it."

Chapter Ten

"I clearly remember telling Mom goodbye that day we took off for the lake. Danny honked for me and I flew out the front door. Mom said, 'Wait a minute, I want a hug,' and I ran back to give her a quick squeeze, kissing the air near her cheek. She pulled me to her, held me a few seconds extra and whispered, 'my beautiful grown-up girl…' Releasing me she said, 'Now, you guys be careful.'

"'Sure, Mom, I'll be home about five. We're going to the movie in Lincoln tonight.'

"'We'll see about that when you get home,' Mom called after me.

"I was still laughing at Mom's mock sternness as I climbed into Danny's Jeep without opening the door. Five of us spent the day swimming and eating, playing touch football and working on our tans. It was the middle of June, two weeks past graduation and we were enjoying our last carefree summer before leaving for college. We were all going to different schools and wanted to cram in as much together-time as possible.

"There weren't many other people at the lake that day, I guess because it was a Thursday. Anyway, the little beach area has a rock that juts out over the water. It's called Pelican's Beak, because of the shape of the bluff. It's about eight feet high and we were jumping and diving, practicing our styles. I had been going off feet first or doing cannonballs. The diving looked like fun, but I wasn't sure the water was deep enough for a dive because a couple of times when I jumped in my toes scraped the bottom. But everyone else had done it without problems, so just before we left I said, 'I really don't want to go home without diving off Pelican's Beak.'

" 'The trick is to arch your back just as you hit the water,' Danny said. 'Start your move upward right away. The most you can get is a skinned knee.' Danny was considered the champion diver of the group so I figured he knew. I climbed up while they all chanted, 'Go, Eve.' I struck my dramatic Olympic-diver pose and took the leap.

"I don't know what went wrong, because that's the last thing I remember until I woke up in the hospital a couple of days later. There was a knot on my head, so I probably hit bottom. But the real damage was to my spine. Nearly every disk was bruised or chipped, with severe injury to my spinal cord just below the waist. I was in traction for several months and had four surgeries to repair all the damaged vertebrae. Of course spinal cord injuries can't be fixed, so here I am…"

Eve leaned forward and took a cookie off the plate. The two women nibbled in silence, then Eve spoke again.

"But, what I really want to tell you about is what happened to me during those months in the hospital. A few days after the accident all the doctors gathered in my room with my parents, and I heard the news about how I'd be spending my life in a wheelchair. And about how lucky I was to have full use of my upper body. How I would still be able to live a very full life because of all the help out there for the disabled…" She took a deep breath. "Well, the next morning, I lay there staring at the ceiling, an oxygen tube helping me breathe, an IV in my arm feeding me and a catheter draining out the leftovers. I heard a vaguely familiar voice from the door.

" 'Eve! Hi! I heard you were up here on Four.'

"I looked toward the chirpy voice and saw Belinda Lark, a junior from Newton High, who sat behind me in choir. She had a great voice and took a lot of teasing about her name. She stood there, wearing a pink Candy Striper uniform, and I said, rather stupidly, 'Belinda? What are you doing here?'

" 'I volunteer a couple of days a week. When I was fourteen and too young to get a job, Mom arranged this to give me something to do. And it turned out I really enjoy it. So even though I have a job at McDonald's now I still come when I can.'

" 'What do you do here?'

" 'Oh, take magazines and the candy cart around, and sometimes I get to read to the sick kids upstairs or work in the gift shop. Just plug in wherever I'm needed.'

"For the next half-hour Belinda rattled on about her job and school and the last movie she'd seen. From then on, she came back every time she was in the hospital. I really looked forward to her visits and finally she began coming every day, even when she wasn't scheduled to work as a Candy Striper. She always brought news or gossip about the goings-on with the kids in Newton.

"Once, while she was helping me sit up, she pulled back the covers to adjust my legs. She sort of recoiled and said, 'My gosh, girl, when was the last time you shaved?'

" 'Well, duh, that would be June 13, the day of the accident.'

" 'The hair here is about an inch long. How can you stand it?'

" 'Hello. I can't feel it.' We both fell out laughing then. Right away she got one of those little kits they hand out to new patients and used the razor to make my legs all smooth and sexy. Then she braided my hair. From then on, she kept me looking good even when I felt lousy.

"When I was lying on my face after surgery, she read to me, everything from Seventeen to Steven King. She offered to read the Bible, but I told her I'm not much of a Bible reader. Then, one day when we were talking she said something about figuring out how all this fit into The Plan.

" 'What do you mean, The Plan?' I asked her.

" 'Well, in Jeremiah it says God has a plan for us…'

" 'Great, so God's plan is for me to break my back and spend my life in this bed.'

" 'No, his plan is…' She reached into her backpack and pulled out a dog-eared book, flipped through the pages and read out loud, 'Jeremiah 29:11. I alone know the plans I have for you, plans to bring you prosperity and not disaster, plans to bring about the future you hope for.' She shut the book. 'See, his plan for you is *prosperity*, not disaster. His plan is *good*. We just wonder how all this fits into it.'

" 'Yeah, well, I sure do wonder that.'

" 'The main thing for you to do now is just *know* it fits and that even though your life may be different from what *you* planned, it can still have all the good that *God* planned.'

"Just then, she was interrupted by a nurse or someone, but the seed was planted. I thought about that conversation a lot and began to hold on to it. I was raised in the Catholic Church but really hadn't gone very deep with my religion. I did all the things I should, said my rosary, took communion, made confession and did my penance, but I was mostly going through the motions without knowing why. My faith had never been tested. Certainly not to this degree.

"After school started, Belinda couldn't make it to the hospital every day, but she came three or four times a week and she was amazing. Mom and Dad were there all the time, but most everyone else had drifted away, gone off to college or wherever to continue their lives. Belinda and I became best friends in a way I never could have believed possible. I took so much more than I gave, or at least it felt like that to me. But she never acted as though our friendship was one-sided or that there was anything unusual about it at all. We laughed and talked and gossiped and discussed developments on our favorite sit-coms. I came home from the hospital about the time she was taking the ACT. She made a 28 and was so excited. She planned to go to UN Lincoln and major in pre-med.

" 'Maybe we can go to school together,' she said one day. When I just stared at her without answering she went on. 'Don't worry, they give the ACT again in the spring, if you think you need to take it again.'

" 'What are you talking about? I can't go to school.'

" 'Sure you can. If your family is broke there's always scholarships and loans…'

" 'We're not broke. At least I don't think so.'

" 'Then what's your problem?'

" 'Belinda, if you haven't noticed, I'm in a wheelchair.'

" 'So?'

" 'So how do I get around a campus?'

" 'Good grief, haven't you noticed all those ramps? Your mom probably won't want you to live in the dorm the first year anyway, and I'm only taking twelve hours the first semester, so we could get our schedules to match and commute together. It would be *fun!*'

" 'I know it would be fun. I just never thought about it being possible.'

" 'With God all things are possible.'

"That's something different about Belinda. She quotes Bible verses like someone else might quote Shakespeare or Charlie Brown. She does it so naturally. I don't know how to explain it, but she says a scripture in a conversational manner and you just know that book is something she lives by and applies to everything she does. You don't get the feeling she's doing it for effect. She doesn't follow the quote with a chapter and verse reference. Like no one quotes a Charlie Brown wisdom and then says 'the New York Times, April 1999', do they?"

Sharon had been listening intently as Eve talked non-stop, and the pause after the question caught her by surprise. "Well, no, I guess they don't. Belinda sounds like a unique person. So you started school together?"

"Yes. I got it done, the ACT and all the entrance exams and paper work. Mom and Dad were supportive but very protective. Mom drove us to Lincoln three days a week the first semester. I think she was afraid to let me out of her sight. I decided to major in pre-law. I had thought about being a lawyer … I love *The Practice* and *Law and Order* … and my dancing career is pretty well shot. Our commuting together works fine. We're thinking about living on campus next year. Belinda wants to get into med school in Omaha and I plan to apply to several graduate schools so I don't know where I'll be. Of course, Mom and Dad want me to stay close to home.

"When all of this fell together, I began to think maybe God *does* have a plan for my life and *is* going to help me work it out. Then something happened that brought me face to face with difficulty. Since my accident someone had always been around to take care of me, Mom, Dad, Belinda, nurses, physical therapists. But one night, the reality of my helplessness crashed in.

"Last semester I talked Mom into letting me take a night class. It was my first big independent move. She drove me over and dropped me off in front of the Fine Arts Building, then she went to a movie or the mall. I have a bag that hangs on the chair to carry all my stuff, books, pens, cell phone and so on. After class I would roll across campus, about a block, to the library and either study or hang out with friends. When I was ready to go I'd call Mom and she would come pick me up. It was wonderful to move around on my own.

"Then one night I was tooling down the sidewalk on my way to the library and a wheel hit a rock or a crack in the walk and I veered into the grass. Right at that spot the ground sloped and the chair tipped over and I fell out. My bag spilled all over the place and the chair landed on its side. I ended up halfway on my side and back, my head at the lower end of the incline.

"It was a little after eight o'clock and most of the walking traffic had died down. Probably no one had seen me fall. I yelled for help, but with the wind knocked out of me, the sound I brought out was sort of puny. If I rolled over on my back I could yell louder, but I would be stuck there looking at the trees. On my stomach, I could pull myself around a little using my elbows, though dragging the dead weight of my legs was hard work.

"The path along there was well-lit, but I had landed off the path, near a bush in the dark. I knew my best chance of speedy rescue was my cell phone, so I rolled over on my stomach in order to reach around and find it. I don't know how long I rooted around in the grass, feeling for that phone. I'd stretch out as far as I could, pat the ground, then inch forward a little and try again. I was aware that my cell could be somewhere under my lower body and I'd never know it.

"On about the tenth try of scooting and feeling around, I found my book bag and located my phone beside it. Excited, I pulled it to my face to punch in Mom's number. Then I realized the battery had fallen out. The phone was useless. I lay my head on my arms and just cried. I had worked so hard to take care of myself. This shouldn't happen to me. Now, I might be stuck all night. Unless I somehow found the battery and could figure out how to re-install the thing, while propped on my elbows. The task seemed impossible.

"Then I remembered what Belinda said about how, with God, all things are possible. Lying there with my face in the dirt the only prayer I could come up with was 'God, help me.'

"I raised my head. I heard something! The steady slap of sneakers on the cement walk. *A jogger! He's going to run right by. Will he see me? Yell – LOUD! I hope he doesn't have on earphones…* 'HELP!'

"He saw me. I was saved. Believe me, I thanked God for that jogger. And from that moment on I have diligently searched for the meaning and purpose in my life. I know it's real and right now with school and all, the plan seems to be for me to prepare for the future. While I do that, I am also trying to spend time with God every day, getting to know Him better.

"I don't know if God wants me to be a public defender or a good Christian D.A. Sometimes it feels like I'll be the last to know His plan. And I don't know if you believe God would answer a prayer that was only two words long, but I do."

"When those two words are 'help me'? Yes. I can believe that," Sharon said.

CHAPTER ELEVEN

Date: April 2, 2004

From: biggirlnow

To: sjordan

Sharon: I enjoyed our visit so much. I feel like I've finally met the sister I've always wanted. Mom said to tell you she's sorry you two didn't meet but she thought we might need some privacy. Maybe next time. And I hope there will be a next time and that all our talk about keeping in touch is something we really mean.

Love, Eve

Date: April 3, 2004

From: sjordan

To: biggirlnow

Eve: Of course we'll keep in touch. I want that. Let me know how things are going in school and I'll tell you all the exciting details of my life. Ha ha.

Love, Sharon

Date: April 3, 2004
From: sjordan
To: roger.johnson

Dear Lt. Johnson,

Thank you for your kindness at the Visitor's Center. It was nice to see a friendly face. I made it to Newton and back to the airport just fine. Thanks again for your help.

Sincerely,
Sharon Jordan

Date: April 10, 2004
From: roger.johnson
To: sjordan

Dear Sharon:

And thank *you* for your kind words. I hope you are enjoying the beautiful spring weather as much as we are and that the dogwood in Arkansas is as beautiful as it is here.
Regards, Roger

Date: April 20, 2004
From: biggirlnow
To: sjordan

Hi Sharon: Just had to write to give you the news. Mom and I drove over to UN Lincoln to look at rooms! They have just remodeled the dorm for people in wheelchairs. The whole place has ramps and lifts and emergency call buttons. (That makes Mom feel better.) So it looks like it will happen in September! I'll be on my own at school. This is absolutely the most exciting thing ever. Maybe next year I'll get a VAN! Write me back.

Love, Eve

Date: April 22, 2004
From: sjordan
To: biggirlnow

Omigosh! I can't believe it. How thrilled you must be, though I understand your mom's concern. What did you call me? Big sister? I guess I'm old enough to understand your mom's worry but young enough to remember the feeling of being on my own. (I'm an only kid, too.) Congratulations. Eve, since talking to you, I have thought a lot about my purpose in life. I have always drifted, or let whatever wind blow me along, with no consideration of the meaning of life or what I should be doing with my time on earth. I'm looking into different kinds of volunteer work. Surely I'm supposed to be doing something useful.
Love, Sharon

Date: May 1, 2004
From: biggirlnow
To: sjordan

Sharon: Go for it. You have nothing to lose. Even if the project you pursue is not exactly what God planned, you'll be giving something back to society. How can that be wrong?
Love, Eve

Date: May 15, 2004
From: roger.johnson
To: sjordan

Dear Sharon: Are you by any chance an Arkansas Razorback fan? I love to watch football, but I must confess I have no idea about how the college draft system works. There's a senior from one of the Lincoln high schools who, rumor has it, is being courted by Arkansas. Of course everyone in Nebraska hoped he would go to school here. But instead your team may be getting a hot shot linebacker.
Roger

Date: May 25, 2004
From: sjordan
To: roger.johnson

Everyone who lives in Arkansas is a Razorback fan. Seriously, it is impossible to ignore what's happening on the sports scene in Fayetteville year round. However, I read that your young man decided to be a Cornhusker after all.
Sharon

Date: June 3, 2004
From: biggirlnow
To: sjordan

Hi Sharon, Things are moving along here in Newton. While I'm at home this summer I'm getting everything lined up for my independent living. We're interviewing caregivers. I need someone to come by

every morning and night to get me in and out of bed. How did the blood drive go? You said you were helping. What did you do? (eeeoou!)
Love, Eve

Date: June 10, 2004
From: sjordan
To: biggirlnow

Silly. I didn't draw blood. I registered the people who came and I gave out orange juice to the donors. Next week the Chamber of Commerce is sponsoring a health fair and I volunteered to help staff the Red Cross booth. I am also captain of the neighborhood recycling team. I'm staying very active and I suppose it's all worthwhile. And it keeps me from thinking about how much I miss Tim.
Love, Sharon

Date: June 20, 2004
From: biggirlnow
To: sjordan

I understand why you don't want to think about missing Tim. It hurts. But do you think avoiding it is a good idea?
Love, Eve

Date: July 4, 2004
From: roger.johnson
To: sjordan

Dear Sharon, Happy Independence Day. Did I ever tell you I have a six-year-old son? My wife died when Todd was a baby and we live here with my mom. I don't know why I'm telling you this now, but today was a day of picnics and fireworks and for some reason I thought of you. Hope you are doing well.
Regards, Roger

Date: July 10, 2004
From: sjordan
To: roger.johnson

Fireworks here too and a parade. Burnsville is a small town that has held onto some of the old traditions, including the election of Miss Firecracker. But it's all fun for the kids, huh?

I guess I didn't know you had a son. Todd is a nice name. We really haven't talked about our personal lives, have we? Though you know a lot about mine, I suppose.
Sharon

Date: August 1, 2004

From: sjordan

To: biggirlnow

Hi Eve, Getting close to school, isn't it? I know you're excited. Jerry Thompson (the pastor here) put me onto a new volunteer effort I'm really interested in. There's a group from Burnsville that goes to Little Rock one Sunday a month to serve lunch in the basement of a little church close to downtown. Homeless people can come by and get a meal. I tagged along last Sunday and it really felt like I was putting my time and energy to good use. We'll see how it goes. Got a letter today inviting me to a grief support group. Probably won't go. I'm doing okay. More later.

Love, Sharon

Chapter Twelve

Sharon pulled into the parking lot of the Methodist Church, noting the few cars already there. *I'm not sure this is my cup of tea.* She turned off the motor and opened the door. *Of course nothing says I have to stay if this whole thing creeps me out.* Initially she had tossed aside the notice from the pastor about the grief support group. But at the urging of her mother and Eve, she had agreed to attend the first session.

She glanced again at the letter lying on the seat beside her, "…several losses in our church family this past year. Tim's death was a tragedy to all of us … gather together to support each other and to find closure … group will meet for six to eight weeks… If it seems this would meet your needs, please come…"

Closure. That word again. *Everyone tells me I need to find it. To get on with my life. The thought is ludicrous.* She found herself feeling more than a little irritated when some well-meaning person voiced a platitude. *If I hear he's in a better place one more time, I'll scream… Golly, maybe I do need some help.*

The group gathered in the church parlor, furnished by the United Methodist Women with comfortable chairs and end tables holding lamps that gave out a soft, homey glow. A short blonde forty-ish woman greeted each one as they entered.

"Hi, I'm Patti."

"Sharon Jordan." She extended her hand.

"Hi, Sharon. Just sit anywhere. Do you know any of the others?"

"No, I don't think so."

"That's okay. We'll get acquainted later."

Sharon sat in a maroon wingback chair next to a table bearing a brass plaque inscribed, 'in memory of Beulah Anderson.' Another on the base of the lamp held a similar message, though Sharon couldn't make out the name without leaning in closer. *Which I'm not just about to do.*

She looked around. *I think this is the room where my family gathered before Tim's funeral. I was in such a fog, I didn't pay attention.*

Patti, who turned out to be Patricia Norman, Licensed Clinical Social Worker, introduced herself to the group of two men and five women seated in the circle. She announced that they would have a coffee break later in another room, then she outlined the ground rules for the sessions.

"In a group like this, whatever is said here, stays here. We all have to feel that this is a safe place to say anything we want. Sometimes the death of someone we love brings out a lot of negative feelings. If you want to express anger, resentment or whatever comes up, this is the place you should be able to do that. When one is talking, the rest of us listen. We don't have side conversations and we don't interrupt to share insight or give unsolicited advice. The goal of the group is to be supportive while each person works through his or her issues.

"At a later time, we'll hear everyone's story about their personal loss. But, tonight, let's introduce ourselves and simply say, '...my father/sister/significant other died however-long-ago.' Now, don't worry and don't be surprised if saying this aloud brings on a few tears. That's not unusual, even though you may think you're past that."

Along with Sharon there were two more widows; another woman and one of the men had each lost a parent. The other man's twin sister died suddenly a year ago and the last woman's fiancé was killed in Afghanistan. Each made their opening statement tentatively, as though testing the water in a hot bath. Sharon felt grateful that when she said, "I'm Sharon. My husband died six months ago," her voice trembled only slightly.

Next, Patti asked questions randomly, drawing out the members of the group, gently respecting the ones who still seemed fragile. An older woman, Myrna, had been the primary caregiver for her husband who died after a long illness. Her only child lived in California. She had never worked outside her home. Claire, whose father died two years ago, was a native of Australia and had no relatives in this country. *Two years and still no closure?*

"Sharon, your husband died six months ago? Was it sudden?"

"Yes, a car wreck."

"I'm so sorry. Do you have children?"

Sharon felt a choking sensation. Her eyes stung. She struggled to keep her voice level.

"No, we were trying." She bent quickly to dig through her purse for a tissue, not noticing that every end table in the room sported a decorative box. Suddenly, tears flowed freely and unbidden. She couldn't speak. She leaned forward, elbows on her knees, face buried in her hands, and sobbed.

Several minutes passed. Patti lay her hand lightly on Sharon's shoulder and waved to the others to move out to the coffee break area. Sharon was faintly aware of the comforting touch. She paid no attention to the slight rustling as the group left the room. Spent with sadness, she raised her head. She and Patti were alone.

"I'm sorry," Sharon said, "I don't know where that came from."

"Really?"

"Really. I've been doing very well. Early on, when I had to tell someone … someone who didn't know … that Tim … was … is gone … I might just burst into tears unexpectedly. I couldn't seem to say the words out loud without getting emotional. Why did saying we had no children bring on such a flood?"

"Perhaps this is an area that is still painful to you."

"I admit I haven't thought much about … well … I suppose now the chance of my having children is slim." She pulled a tissue from the nearest box.

"Even if I married again … and I can't imagine that … I'll soon be too old for child bearing. I'll never love anyone like I loved Tim. You didn't know him. He was a wonderful person. I miss him terribly. But I thought I had moved forward … accepted what happened."

"I'm sure you have. This is something new. You're grieving for your child."

Sharon gaped at Patti as the truth soaked in. Then her face crumpled and again she wept uncontrollably as she had the day Tim died, when she lay curled up on their bed. She had cried that day for Tim – ripped from her arms. Now, it was for their child – stolen from her womb.

Patti sat silently, her hand still resting on Sharon's shoulder, until the tears dissolved into a convulsive sigh. Only then did she speak.

"You've taken a huge step tonight, Sharon. And I know it's painful. I hope you'll come back next week. I think as you hear the others' stories you'll realize you're not alone in all this. No one's situation is exactly like yours, but their pain is much the same. It just came about in a different way. Hearing their struggles will help you with yours. Help you gain closure."

How can I have closure around something I'll miss the rest of my life. I'll never take a child to the first day of kindergarten, never stand with pride at a graduation ceremony, never be mother of the bride or groom … no grandchildren… They say no one ever recovers from the loss of a child. I believe them.

CHAPTER THIRTEEN

Entering her house an hour later, Sharon felt a fatigue never known before in her life. The days after Tim's death, when she had so much to do and slept so poorly, she would fall into bed at night bone-tired. But this was different. Her *soul* felt weary.

She walked to the office room and turned on the computer. Before Tim's death she had used email only for business purposes. But after returning from Nebraska, she enjoyed keeping in touch with Eve online and found her casual exchanges with Roger Johnson interesting. Now, at the end of each day, Sharon looked forward to messages from her email friends.

No mail tonight. She felt a twinge of disappointment at the empty mail box. She sat down and, on a whim, typed in Roger's address.

Date: September 7, 2004
From: sjordan
To: roger.johnson

Did you attend a grief support group after your wife died? Tonight I went to a group being organized at the church and the strangest thing happened. I know we haven't talked about personal things and I don't want to be intrusive, but I sure would like to process this with someone. Okay?

Sharon

She read the message over three times, changing a word here and there, before finally clicking 'send.' She left the office, walked through the den and out onto the deck. The evening air was only slightly cooler than during the day. Stars shown brightly against the black sky. *Here it is September and hot as July. We'll probably have a mild winter. Not that I would know. Born and raised in Arkansas but I still don't know how to read the wooly worms.*

She returned inside and, after securing the outside doors, stepped into the shower. Ready for bed, she went into the office to turn off the computer. To her surprise, there was an answer from Roger.

Date: September 7, 2004
From: roger.johnson
To: sjordan

Yes, I did, and found it helpful. I had a lot of anger about her death. I thought the doctors could have prevented it. Anyway, I encourage you to stick with the group.

Hmm. I don't even know how she died. I assumed a disease, cancer or something. He said his little boy – Todd, is it? – was a baby. She scrolled down to read the rest of the message.

Sharon, I would like to talk to you more about this. I haven't mentioned it before because I wasn't sure, but I will be attending a Law Enforcement seminar in Little Rock the first week in October.

I'm not sure where Burnsville is from there, but do you suppose we could meet and have dinner or something? I would really like to see you again.

Think about it and let me know.

R.

Chapter Fourteen

Sharon slid the heaping dishes of chicken, mashed potatoes and fried okra onto the counter as Carol Matthews chatted away about a new project she had in mind. Carol headed up the volunteers from Burnsville First Methodist who came to Little Rock once a month to serve lunch to the homeless. Each Sunday, Fifth Street Methodist, an old church located near the downtown area, opened its basement Fellowship Hall to forty or more hungry souls who came for a free meal. Larger churches in the suburbs and surrounding towns furnished the food.

"I was talking to Brother Thompson," Carol went on, "about opening a food pantry and clothes closet in Burnsville. We can get food subsidies from the Rice Depot and distribute it in our area. Lots of poor folks live in our county. I think it would meet a real need. What do you think?"

Sharon, only half listening, said, "Sounds good."

"Of course if we did that, we'd probably have to drop this. I promised my family I wouldn't take on anything else without letting something go."

"Oh. But this is a real need too, isn't it?"

"Sure, none of the free lunch places are open on the weekend. Don't know what these people do on Saturday but several of the churches see to it they eat on Sunday."

Sharon glanced at Carol, a small frown wrinkling her forehead. *These people? Sort of politically incorrect...*

"So what will happen if we stop bringing food?" Sharon asked.

"Oh, I imagine they'll find some other church to take our place. I enjoyed setting up this program, but it's going well now. I guess the challenge is gone. I'm ready to move on to other things."

Their conversation ended as Neil Matthews, Carol's husband, opened the doors. Men, women and a few children crowded in and formed a line that reached from the kitchen to the outside door. Each person received a generous helping of chicken and vegetables and a choice of coffee, tea or water, then took their food to the long banquet tables. They ate quickly with little conversation.

"Can I take a plate for my friend?" The woman standing at the counter appeared fragile and weather-beaten, her cropped hair plastered to her head. She wore faded jeans and a tee shirt with 'Opryland USA' emblazoned across the front.

Carol glanced up. "After everyone's been served you can come back for seconds."

The woman moved on and Carol leaned toward Sharon, muttering under her breath, "Odds are there is no friend. She's just trying to hoard for later."

Sharon took a pitcher of tea into the dining room to offer refills. Ben Adams, pastor of Fifth Street church, encouraged volunteers to mix with the visitors. He said the serving counter shouldn't appear to be a line drawn between the 'haves' and the 'have-nots.'

"Would you like more tea?" Sharon approached a man sitting at the end of one of the tables, as alone as possible in a room full of people. She couldn't guess his age. The face under the scraggly beard could have been any age between thirty and sixty.

"Yes, please." He did not offer his glass, but rather reached down and pulled off a filthy sneaker, flexing his foot. Sharon steeled herself against the urge to step back.

" 'Scuse me ma'am. I have a huge blister on my heel that is killing me."

"Oh. I'm sorry."

"Yeah, it hurts like the very Devil."

"Gosh, I know how you feel."

The man's head jerked up sharply. "Do you really? Do you mean that you know how I feel because once you got a blister on your dainty little foot when you wore a brand new pair of hundred dollar shoes? Or do you *really* know how I feel because you've had on the same pair of socks for a week and just walked five miles to get here? Because the last thing you had to eat was half a hamburger you found in McDonald's Dumpster yesterday."

Sharon stared at the man. She could think of nothing to say. He gave a snort.

"I get so sick of you snooty church-lady types who feel so good about yourselves because you give us a piece of chicken." The man hadn't raised his voice but Sharon was acutely aware of the people sitting at the nearby tables. She knew they could hear what was going on.

"I'll bet you've been spoiled and pampered all your life. I'll bet you don't know how it feels to have your family say they don't want to see you, so don't bother to come home."

Sharon found her voice. "You have no ri…"

"That's the truth, Lady. I have no rights. Anytime the former President comes to town bringing his fancy friends, the city fathers try to get rid of us, tear up our camps, shuffle us off somewhere where we can't be seen." He snorted again. "Like he doesn't know people live under that bridge."

"I'm sorry, I…"

"Save your sorrys and save your pity. But thanks for the chicken, anyway." With that he stuck his shoe under one arm, picked up his plate and cup and limped through the maze of tables and out the door.

Sharon stood, shaking from the encounter. Neil came up behind her. "Are you all right?"

An old man at the next table spoke up. "Don't mind George. He had a bad night and he's just pissed off … excuse me, Ma'am. We 'preciate the food. Really."

"It's all right. I'm okay. Do you want more tea?" She squared her shoulders and lifted her chin. *I will not cry.* She filled more glasses around the room then retreated to help with clean-up.

Later, in the van, Carol slipped into the seat next to her. "Don't let it bother you," she said. "He had no right to speak to you like that. Some of these people are so ungrateful."

Sharon cringed at the words. "No, that was a thoughtless thing I said. We say we know how people feel when we haven't a clue. He just called me on it."

She turned away from Carol and looked out the window.

I should know better than to offer empty platitudes. How many times in the last six months has it happened to me? I've been irritated at the superficial sympathy people offer while my whole life falls apart. The only ones who really understand are the folks in that support group. I'd have to live in a box down by the river to really know how that man feels.

He's right about one thing, I've had it soft. Until Tim died I never did anything I didn't want to do. Life's been easy. I had no idea how easy until it all changed.

Carol moved across the aisle to talk to someone else, leaving a grateful Sharon with her own thoughts. *Eve says God helps her when she asks. Maybe the man should ask God to help. Maybe I should have suggested that. Is that what they call witnessing? I have a feeling it would have made him even madder.*

Something in her head clicked, connecting with a directive she heard every Sunday she attended church: 'Pray for those who are in need.' *I'll ask for him. I've never prayed for someone I don't know, much less for someone I don't even like very much. So if he doesn't ask for himself…*

She leaned against the head rest and took a deep breath. *Dear God, help this man. I don't know his name … oh, yes, it's George. I don't know what he might need from you … maybe to reconcile with his family … maybe to find a job or a home. But you know. So please help him.*

Back in Burnsville, the van pulled into the church's parking lot. Sharon waved good-bye to the others, started her car and turned toward home, only slightly aware of the change that had come to her life.

Chapter Fifteen

Sharon liked what was happening to downtown Little Rock. After the opening of the new Clinton Presidential Library last year, the River Market area blossomed with the ensuing tourist trade. *If they ever finish the construction and street repair, it'll be lovely.*

The site of the Law Enforcement Seminar was the State House Convention Center next to the Peabody Hotel. Sharon agreed to meet Roger Johnson in the hotel lobby in time for dinner in the Capricco Steakhouse.

As she neared the downtown exit, Sharon realized she had an hour to kill before dinner, so she decided to circle the city and cross the bridges that spanned the Arkansas River. At one pass-over she spied what looked like a pile of debris under the shelter of the concrete abutment on the opposite side of the river. She slowed as much as she dared to peer at the array of tent-like structures. Wooden crates, the size that might have once held large appliances, had been fashioned into make-shift shelters. Blankets hung over the open end of some of the boxes, providing whatever small amount of privacy might be available.

She took the next exit and backtracked, trying to find a service road or street that traveled along the riverbank. She passed a row of run-down apartment buildings, the outside walls decorated with spray-painted symbols she could only guess was gang graffiti. She turned at the next corner, hoping to circle the block and head out of the neighborhood. She realized almost instantly that she had entered a dead-end street. Ahead of her stood a vacant building. Two men lounged against an old car in the otherwise empty parking lot and Sharon watched in amazement as one handed over what looked to be folded bills and received in return a small package from the other man's pocket. *I just saw a drug deal go down!*

Thankful for the automatic door locks on her car, she whipped a U-turn in the middle of the block and headed back the way she had come, looking for signs indicating which street back to the on-ramp. *I guess the homeless man was right after all. I'm not brave enough to get a close-up look at how other people live.*

She left her car with the parking valet and walked into the hotel, looking for Roger.

"Sharon!" He strode across the plush carpet and grabbed her hand.

Dressed in a business suit rather than a police uniform and sidearm, Roger looked different than she remembered. *He's really quite tall. And I didn't notice that his hair is thin. And graying. Wonder how old he is?*

"Hi, thanks for coming." He continued to shake her hand. "It's good to see you again."

"Hello, Roger, how've you been?"

"Good, good. Let's get our table and then we can talk."

Sharon encouraged Roger to try the sweet tea, a specialty in Arkansas restaurants. After the waiter delivered drinks and took their orders, Roger looked at Sharon.

"So, tell me, how are you? Things going okay?"

"Yes. Fine. I'm staying busy."

"How is the support group working out?"

"Very well. I wasn't sure at first if I wanted to do that … you know … discuss my feelings with strangers. But, it's weird, they don't seem like strangers. I guess it's because I feel like they completely understand what I'm talking about."

"They do. That's the whole idea."

"I thought that no one could possibly understand how hurt I was, because no one else had suffered like I had. The circumstances around Tim's death made my grief worse than anyone else's could possibly be. Or so I thought."

"And…?"

"Well, there are people there whose stories are just as tragic as mine. My attitude of 'My hurt is worse than yours' sounds pretty childish, now."

"I think it's part of what they call the stages of grief."

"I guess so. You said you attended a group after your wife died?"

"Yes. I had a lot of anger. I thought with better medical care Liz might have lived."

"What happened?"

"When Todd was three months old, she found a lump in her breast. The doctor said it was probably a swollen milk gland and that we should watch it. So we watched it … grow." He took a sip of tea, looked into his glass. "Man, that's sweet. Anyway, six months later they removed the lump, which had grown from the size of a pea to the size of a marble. Malignant, of course. She spent the next year in treatment and died when Todd was twenty months old."

"I'm so sorry."

"I had been in the narcotics division … really exciting work. When Liz got sick, I transferred to traffic. Safer duty, more regular hours."

Sharon looked at him across the table, sipped her water.

"You know," Roger went on, "I felt angry because my life was not what I had planned it would be. I was angry that Todd would never know what a wonderful mother he had. Angry that he has to be raised by a senior-citizen grandma and I'm a part-time dad." He idly moved the array of silverware on each side of his plate. Then he looked at Sharon and smiled.

"But, I'm over all that now."

Sharon gave a wry laugh. "I can see you are."

"No, really. I know sometimes I don't sound like it, but … I can see … I try to see …" He cleared his throat. "Are you a Christian?"

"What?"

"Well, uh, I just wondered if … you … well … sometimes I get some help from that."

Sharon couldn't help but smile. *You either get tongue-twisted or put your foot in your mouth. Cute. And I'm inclined to give you a break.*

Conversation paused while the waiter served their food and refilled their drinks. During the silence, Sharon had an idea.

"Roger, I would like your help with something."

"Anything. What did you have in mind?"

"Well, to give a little background, a few weeks ago, I met a homeless man."

"You what?"

Sharon told him about the encounter at the Fifth Street Methodist free lunch program. Roger listened attentively as she described George's outburst and smiled as she recounted her prayer in the van, asking God to help the unknown man.

"So, I figured there was no other way to help him but ask God to do it for me."

"That's right. You did the right thing. All you could do."

"Yes, but since then, something exciting has happened. I tried it again and it worked."

"Tried what again?"

"Praying for people. Every Sunday there's a list in the church bulletin. So, I take it home and say a little prayer for these people I know only slightly, if at all."

"Okay. That's good."

"No, you don't understand. I've gotten results! No kidding, there was this woman going for tests, and I prayed for her and they turned out benign. And someone in the support group needed a job and she found one the very next week. And ... and ... there were several other instances like that."

Roger smiled. "Sharon, that's wonderful. It's a joy when we see our prayers answered."

"Don't pat me on the head, Roger. I'm not a child. I realize that for some unknown reason, it doesn't always work. And a lot of times, we have no way of knowing if it worked or not. But I'd like to follow up on something and I can do that better if you help me."

"Help you what?"

"I want to see if my prayer helped that homeless man. Maybe now he has a job and a home. Maybe he reconnected with his family. Heck, maybe he just got a new pair of shoes or some clean socks. I want to know."

"Sharon, I don't know what it is you want me to do."

"Well, he said something about living in a box under a bridge. I tried to drive down to where I thought that might be..."

She stopped as Roger's fork dropped from his hand, bounced off his plate and hit the floor. The waiter appeared from nowhere, replaced the utensil and retreated silently.

"Sharon, I hope you're kidding me."

"No. I went down there, but I'm ashamed to admit, I chickened out. The neighborhood is a little creepy and when it comes right down to it, I'm not sure how to find him."

"When did you do this?"

"Earlier today, before I came here."

"And did it occur to you that some gang member might think he had struck pay dirt when he saw a nicely dressed woman in a good car?"

"No. I guess I didn't think it through very well. But with you to help me..."

"Help you what?"

"Will you stop saying that? Help me find that man. I want to see if my prayer had any affect on him at all."

"First, if I were willing to do that ... which I'm not ... how would you go about choosing just the right box city? I'd be willing to bet there's one under every bridge in Little Rock. I don't know anything about this town. I wouldn't know where to start."

"Yes, we might not find him on the first try."

"Do you even know his name?"

"Someone at the church called him George."

"So we just walk under every bridge in the city yelling, 'Hey, George, there's a crazy lady who wants to talk to you.' Is that the plan?"

"No need to be sarcastic."

"Sharon, do you have any concept of how dangerous this is?"

"Why would anyone want to hurt me?"

"Oh, I don't know ... to take your money, your car ... your LIFE, just to stay in practice!"

"Okay, if you don't want to help me..."

"Wait a minute. I want you to promise you won't go down there. Look, you said he was an angry person. Can't you see that he just might not be thrilled to see you? He might think you were interfering ... might be hostile. *Please,* Sharon."

"I don't know. Maybe you're right..."

"I've got an idea. Why don't you check out the free lunch thing again? If he's there, you can see how he's doing. If he's not there, that could be a sign that he's moved on to better times."

"Maybe. That might work."

"So you promise you won't be looking under bridges?"

"I guess we've already established I'm not brave enough to do that alone."

"Sharon, will you promise me that you won't go there again? Or at least that you'll discuss it with me first?"

"Okay." *Good grief, you sound so protective. Like my parents … or Tim. What's that about?*

CHAPTER SIXTEEN

Date: October 15, 2004

From: sjordan

To: roger.johnson

Roger: At your suggestion I have gone back to Fifth Street's free lunch program several times, but haven't seen the man called George. However, in doing that, I have found other places to focus my prayers. There is a little girl, hardly more than four years old, that I see regularly with a woman I assume is her mother. I pray for that child every day. She deserves a better life. Many adults are homeless because of choices they have made, but that child hasn't had a chance to choose.

Thanks again for dinner. I enjoyed it and our walk around the River Market. And, of course, the good conversation.

Later, Sharon

Date: October 25, 2004

From: sjordan

To: biggirlnow

Hi, Eve: Well, tonight was the last night for the support group and I must admit to a few tears. We grew to be like a family. Now I have two or three people I can call if I need to talk. I found some relief for the grief of losing Tim and I learned a little more about myself. After the first shock, I had to deal with the reality that I will never have a child. Losing Tim ended that dream.

I seriously want to find what I'm supposed to be doing with my life. But I've had a scary thought. What if my purpose in life was to be a mom? What if God's plan for me was that I have a family … be mom to a future president … or brilliant scientist? Now, if that's not going to happen, what? My life has no purpose?

This is something I talked about in the group and began to get a grip on. But, oh, I wanted a baby! I hope that God has a 'plan B' for me. I can't shake the conviction that Tim and I would have been good parents, and the fact that it will never happen brings great sadness.

Hope school is going well and living alone is as exciting as you thought it would be.

Love, S.

Date: October 31, 2004
From: roger.johnson
To: sjordan

Hi Sharon: Thanks for talking to me last night. I was feeling pretty beat and it helped to talk and get some perspective. I really miss the job with Narcotics and even though I transferred out almost seven years ago, I have good friends there and some day would like to get back into that kind of work. It's frustrating and I just needed to vent.

I got off early today so I could pick up Todd at school. We needed to shop for shoes for him and a winter coat. We don't do that together very often ... most of those duties fall to Mom. After shopping we went to Burger King for a kid's meal. It's amazing how much joy one of those cheap toys can bring to a kid. And to the parent who watches the process.

Got to run. Taking Todd to trick or treat. Exciting for a kid. Thanks again for listening.

Roger

Date: November 3, 2004
From: sjordan
To: roger.johnson

I have decided the lunch program is my thing to do! I go every Sunday, even when it's not my turn. And I have taken over organizing the once-a-month visit. The previous leader sort of lost interest, or moved on to other things, and I stepped in rather than give it up. I have become good friends with some of the regulars there, particularly Mary Kay, the woman with the young child I told you about. I found out she isn't homeless after all, but lives in Safe Place, the domestic violence shelter. Its location is confidential, but it's obviously within walking distance. Mary Kay brings Kris (her four-year-old daughter) to Sunday School at Fifth Street Methodist and stays for lunch.

At the shelter, the usual procedure is to get a restraining order against the offender and then help the victim relocate, find a job and generally begin life over. If the abuser is facing charges, then social workers help the victim get through court dates and other legalities. I have no idea where Mary Kay might be in the process. I don't want to ask personal questions. But she is such a brave person and so good with Kris, who is a delightful child. I just want to be a friend to them, if I can.

Well. Thanks for asking. I enjoyed telling you about it.

Sharon

Date: November 10, 2004
From: biggirlnow
To: sjordan

Sharon: Things are going really well, now. I'm 'up and around' after being sick. The doctors say paraplegics have kidney infections a lot. Now I'm on a new med that should help head it off in the future. I need to be more careful about watching for the signs of an infection, like running a temp, because I can't feel the symptoms that should warn me. Anyway I'm back in the dorm, though Mom is having a cow wanting me to move back home so she can smother me. No way!

BTW, Mom and Dad (and me too of course) would love 4 U to come here 4 Thanksgiving. If Ur family wouldn't be 2 lonely w/o U, it would be a chance 4 us 2 spend some time 2-gether and visit face to face. Think about it. We would lv 2 have U. (My new phone will text-message. How do you like the text-message-talk?)

Love, Eve

Date: November 12, 2004
From: sjordan
To: biggirlnow

Thanks for the invitation for Thanksgiving. My parents understand totally why I would love to visit you again. I will fly up Wednesday night and rent a car at the airport to come to Newton. I'll leave your house on Friday. Roger Johnson (I told you about him) wants me to spend Saturday seeing the sights of Lincoln. I don't know what's there. Can it take 24 hours to see? lol (See, I know some shorthand, too.) See you soon, Sharon

Date: November 15, 2004
From: biggirlnow
To: sjordan

Aha! He goes to Little Rock, now you come to Nebraska! What's going on? E.

Date: November 16, 2004
From: sjordan
To: biggirlnow

Stop that! He came to Little Rock on business. We have become friends, that's all. Okay, pretty good friends. We email often and talk on the phone occasionally. Just friends. S.

Date: November 20, 2004

From: roger.johnson

To: sjordan

We're all set. I'll pick you up at 7:00 Friday night at the Avis booth at the airport. It'll save you some money on car rental. But you will be dependent on me for transportation for the next 24 hours. Can you stand that? You are so darned independent, it may be hard on you. Just kidding! When you read this, imagine me smiling as I write.

Roger

Date: November 26, 2004

From biggirlnow

To: sjordan

Sharon, You'll get this email when you get home. THANK YOU for coming. You were more than a Thanksgiving guest. We MUST see each other more often.

Love, Eve

Date: November 27, 2004

From: roger.johnson

To: sjordan

Dearest Sharon, I'm concerned that I frightened you with my abrupt question. My heart was overwhelmed and of course I'm not a smooth talker.

I never believed in love at first sight, but the day I met you, when I walked into my office and you sat there, red nose and puffy eyes, half a box of Kleenex used up … I wanted to take you in my arms and hold you away from the hurt. I thought to myself, 'Are you crazy? This woman's husband just died!' So, fortunately, I didn't act on my inappropriate feelings and a law suit was averted. (Okay, that's a joke.) Then when we met at the Visitor Center, I felt the Lord had arranged that meeting as a wonderful gift to me … and hopefully to you, too.

Maybe I'm talking too much again. But please think about what I said tonight. That's all I ask. Please think about it. And pray about it, too.

Love, Roger

Sharon stared at the computer screen. She pushed the 'print' icon, took the paper from the printer tray and walked into the den. Her eyes moved across the message again and again.

Oh, yes, I'll think about it. How can I think of anything else?

Chapter Seventeen

Pleasant weather had made the Thanksgiving visit enjoyable. Sharon arrived in Newton early and after breakfast Thursday, she helped Oleta Bens put the finishing touches on the holiday dinner. Friday, she and Eve spent the day looking at photo albums Sharon had brought along. Eve chose several pictures and created a collage for her dorm room. They parted with warm hugs and promises to see each other again soon.

Saturday turned out to be another beautiful day. Roger had planned activities down to the minute. They ate brunch at a restaurant in Lincoln's Historic Haymarket District, then spent the afternoon wandering through the galleries and antique shops in turn-of-the-century buildings.

As the shops began to close, the pair returned to Sharon's downtown hotel so she could change. The evening's agenda included dinner atop the Regency and tickets for Lied Center's Johnny Carson Theater. After a quick shower, Sharon donned a long black wool skirt with matching turtleneck and a dark red beaded jacket. Sweeping her hair up off her shoulders, she fastened it with an onyx barrette. She pulled soft tendrils from the clip's grasp to frame her face, and applied a generous amount of hairspray. Her efforts were rewarded with a smile from Roger and the raised eyebrows of a stranger standing across the lobby. Roger had slipped into the men's room to put on a tie, with plans to trade his parka for the jacket hanging in his car.

"I hope you like musicals," Roger said.

"I love them! Which one is it?"

"Carousel."

"My favorite! How did you know?"

"I … uh … I took a shot."

The production of the Rogers & Hammerstein musical left Sharon breathless. The acting company of young professionals was superb. She found herself moved to tears by the familiar story: Billy Bigelow, a bit of a rascal, dying suddenly, leaving Julie pregnant with their child. His spirit returns fifteen years later to see his daughter through a time of difficulty. The character's signature song, '*You'll Never Walk Alone*' resonated throughout the auditorium causing an audible swell of emotion in the crowd. Roger reached for Sharon's hand, holding it until the last note faded and applause erupted.

As they entered the lobby again, Roger's hand on her elbow guided her to a setting of luxurious chairs away from the traffic area.

"Can we talk a minute? I want to ask you something."

"Sure." Sharon sat on the edge of her chair, Roger across from her. He leaned forward.

"I don't know how to say this except to blurt it out. Will you marry me?"

If she had been hit in the stomach, she would not have lost her breath more completely. She expected, 'Can I see you again?' Or maybe even, 'Can I spend the night?' But this out-of-left-field question stunned her. Finally, she found her voice. "I don't know what to say."

Roger smiled. "Say 'yes'?"

"We hardly know each other."

"We can change that."

"Roger … I … I know your son needs a mother…"

"No, Sharon, it's not that. Well, he does, but I would never marry anyone for that reason only. He'll grow up and leave home someday. Then what? No, this is for the long haul. Forever." He paused, looked down at his hands clasped tightly between his knees. "I guess I didn't say … Sharon, I love you."

"How can you? You don't know…"

"I know enough. I've seen how brave you are, what a moral person you are, how you care about other people. And you're a Christian. Our beliefs are alike. We're perfect for each other."

Sharon leaned back and looked at him. *You are a dear. This is very sweet, though astounding.* Aloud, she said, "I had a wonderful time today. I suppose you did, too, and that's where this is coming from. We both are probably a bit lonely for companionship. Let's talk about this later, if you still think it's something to talk about. And if you change your mind, we'll never mention it again and no hard feelings."

Roger stood. "Okay, I can live with that." At the elevator door he pushed the UP button. "You'll get the shuttle okay, tomorrow? Sorry I can't take you to the airport but I really need to get back to work and let some of the other guys take off the rest of the holiday weekend."

"I'll be fine. Thanks for an amazing day."

He raised his hand and fingered a wispy lock of hair falling across her face. Touching her cheek with the tips of his fingers, he bent and kissed her. She stood perfectly still, not responding but not pulling back. He lifted his head and pulled her into his arms and held her. She moved her arms around him, lay her head on his chest and closed her eyes. Never had she felt so content.

***

"You can't be serious!" Sally Seabring reached for the nearest chair and sat down hard, clattering her teacup and spilling a few drops.

Sharon left her mother sitting, walked to the window and looked out at the drizzling rain, taking time to compose her next words. "I haven't decided anything. I just wanted you to know."

"But, surely you can't be thinking of marrying someone you just met! And moving away from Arkansas! Why, we don't even know anybody in Nebraska!"

"Mother, I don't understand your reaction. You and Daddy have always supported anything I wanted."

"I suppose we have, when you were choosing a college, or marrying a nice boy like Tim. But I haven't even met this man. Isn't this the one you were so angry about?"

"I know him better now. He's really quite nice. I know it hasn't been very long, but..."

"But what?"

"Mother, I want to have children. This may be my last chance."

"You can't be serious."

"I wish you would stop saying that because I'm as serious as I know how to be."

"Well, then, just promise me one thing."

"What is that?"

"That you'll pray about it."

Sharon looked at Sally in disbelief. "Mother, in my whole life I have never heard such a suggestion from you. Where did that come from?"

"I ... uh ... I know you have been much more religious since Tim died. I just thought maybe God would give you some guidance here. I realize that when you were growing up we didn't teach you much about God and praying and all ... all ... that. But that doesn't mean I don't believe in it. Go ahead, pray about it and see what kind of answer you get."

Sharon smiled. "You sound pretty sure God will back you up. As a matter of fact, Mother, I welcome your suggestion. And I intend to follow it. Now you promise me one thing."

"What?"

"That if God gives me the go-ahead, you and Daddy will be okay with this and nice to Roger ... and to Todd. Aren't you eager to be grandparents?"

"Of course we are. But, we care most about you and your happiness. Do you really want to raise another woman's child?"

"Mother, sometimes the things that come out of your mouth amaze me."

***

The first day of December dawned cold but Sharon still chose to sit on the deck, the spot where she often came to try her experiments with prayer. She had told Eve of her conversation with Sally, then said, "I've never really talked to God about me. Just other people."

"You mean all this business about looking for God's plan for your life and you haven't *asked* him about it?"

"Well … no … I guess not. You think I should? What if I don't like his answer?"

The winter wind rippled the pages as Sharon read the verse Eve had recommended, "Trust in the Lord with all your heart and lean not on your own understanding. In all your ways acknowledge him and he will direct your paths." She sat with the open Bible on her lap.

Wow! What a promise! And just what I need. Someone to direct me. Her gaze fixed on the leafless maple tree about fifteen feet from the deck. *First of all, Lord, thank you for this beautiful world. I love Arkansas, even in winter. I don't want to leave. But I'm willing to do that if it is your plan for me. It never occurred to me that marriage might be in my future. So, is it? I have no idea how you send messages, but I need to make the best decision for me and Roger and Todd. And any little strangers that might be in our future. I'm asking you to do this. And soon. You know I'm not getting any younger.*

Chapter Eighteen

Date: December 3, 2004

From: sjordan

To: roger.johnson

Hi Roger: It's very cold here today. I've been sitting in the den with a cup of herbal tea enjoying my plants. I moved all the potted plants off the deck into the house for the winter.

I've been thinking about our conversation (and btw thanks for waiting and not pushing). I've decided a couple of things.

First of all, I am approaching the first Christmas without Tim. I'm a little emotional about this. Like I'm feeling my way through a maze. I need to experience this time without anything else on my mind. Tim and I had some traditions around this holiday and I don't know how it's going to be this year without him. Can you just stand back for now and be a friend?

Also, I feel strongly that you and I should know each other better before we think of a step such as marriage. I need to meet your family and you, mine. It's not exactly a deal breaker, but I would like for our families to be supportive if we decide we have a future together.

So. How about New Year's weekend? You and Todd can come here and meet my folks or I can come there. What do you say?
Sharon

Date: December 4, 2004

From: roger.johnson

To: sjordan

I say take all the time you need. I will never change my mind. I love the idea of New Year's weekend, except for one little thing. I have Christmas with Todd, so I need to work New Year's Eve. I wear a pager the whole weekend. Most years I'm lucky and don't have to answer a call, but anyway, that's the deal. So, you'll come here? That would be wonderful.

And can I call you, just to see how you're doing? One more thing and I won't mention it again until next year. I love you.

Roger

PS. Do the plants move back outside in the spring?

The first Saturday in December, Sharon drove to the tree farm. She and Tim had always followed the Southern tradition of putting up a tree early in the season. They would visit Bailey's Christmas Ranch, choose the perfect specimen so Tim could cut it himself. She turned in Bailey's graveled drive and stopped. She sat for a moment, thinking, then made a U-turn and headed back to town.

This is the first compromise. She stopped in the parking lot of the Burnsville Community Center where the Boy Scouts had trees for sale. She chose a tall one and the boy wrestled it into the back of her dad's pickup. *How ridiculous. Who's going to see this tree? Well, I guess the neighbors will. If I host our usual fourth Sunday get-together.* She pulled the truck into her driveway and parked near the deck. In the rearview mirror, she could see nothing but green fir.

Okay, here's the thing. All that was fun because I was with Tim. He loved Christmas. We loved Christmas together. Doing the same things without him would just be sad. And a lot of work. Those were our *traditions. I need to make my own.*

She dragged the tree out of the truck bed and onto the deck. After she maneuvered it into the stand, she spent the rest of the afternoon stringing popcorn and cranberries. She dipped pine cones in honey, rolled them in bird seed and hung them on the tree. Satisfied with her gift to the birds, she went inside.

As the day ended she sat in front of the fire with a pad and pencil. *Tree for the house? Yes, a small one. Maybe artificial. Decorate? Yes, inside. No outside lights. That was fun for Tim, not for me. Host a party? No. Shopping trip to Little Rock? Maybe, if Mother is interested. But no overnight stay at the Peabody with breakfast in bed. Christmas Eve Communion? Yes.*

She looked at her notes, satisfied with her decisions. *Maybe instead of a party here, I'll help with the kids from the shelter. And maybe I'll drive over to Woodbine one Sunday to that Catholic Church that performs the Messiah every year.*

The telephone interrupted her thoughts.

"Hello."

"Hi, Sharon. Roger here. I just called to remind you that *The Nutcracker* is on PBS tomorrow afternoon, in case you want to watch it. How was your day?"

Chapter Nineteen

The Fellowship Hall of Fifth Street Methodist Church appeared festive with red and green paper chains and children's artwork depicting the birth of Jesus. Tonight, the lunchroom for homeless souls had been transformed into the site of a Christmas party for neighborhood children.

Sally and Sharon unloaded an armful of wrapped boxes and headed to the kitchen to help make sandwiches. They had spent the day at the malls and, in addition to their own shopping, bought toys for the gift exchange. This was Sally's first visit to the ministry where Sharon gave so much of her time.

By six o'clock the room began to fill with children and adults, and Sharon spied Kris and Mary Kay as they came through the door.

"Miss Sharon!" The four-year-old ran toward Sharon's open arms, then stopped short as though someone had pulled an emergency brake. "Hi, Miss Sharon. I knew you'd be here."

Oh, you darling. Will you ever feel safe enough to give someone a hug? "Hello, Kris. I'm so glad to see you." She bent and held out her hand palm up. The grinning child gave her a 'low five.' Sharon touched Mary Kay's arm. "How are things going?"

"Pretty well." Haunted eyes looked out from under her shaggy bangs.

Sharon wanted to ask more, but decided to keep their conversation light.

"Oooh, look!" Kris ran across the polished floor to the tall tree laden with Chrismons, ornaments in the shapes of various Christmas symbols. A world of presents rested underneath the generous expanse of evergreen.

"Thank you all for this party for the kids," Mary Kay said. "Kris has been excited all day. I usually get her to nap every afternoon, but today that was out of the question." She glanced over Sharon's shoulder, made a choking sound. "Oh, my God … Ralph!"

Sharon followed Mary Kay's gaze in time to see the man at the door move across the room and scoop Kris up in his arms. Mary Kay reached her daughter a second later. Holding Kris in the crook of his left arm, the man backhanded Mary Kay and she crumpled to the floor.

"I told you that if you tried to take my child away from me, I'd kill you." He pulled a small gun from his jacket as his wife struggled to her feet. "Fine kind of church this is, breaking up a man's family."

He backed toward the exit.

"Sir, there's nothing to be gained by this," Sharon spoke up. Fighting the urge to rush in and grab the child from his arms, she forced herself to move slowly. In her peripheral vision she saw Ben Adams motioning parents away. Sharon stepped forward. "Please let Kris stay and enjoy the Christmas party."

The man stopped. "Who the hell are you?"

"Just a friend. I'm a friend of Kris'. I think you're scaring her."

The man looked briefly at his daughter, as though considering the request. Mary Kay moved unsteadily into position behind Sharon.

The pair inched closer, within an arm's length of the man and child. Sharon held out her hands and said softly, "Come on, Kris, come to me."

She didn't see him raise his hand. She only felt the steel of the gun as he whacked it against her head. She sank on all fours, stunned, staring at the ancient hardwood floor, trying to focus. Above her, she heard the gunshot and a small voice, saying, "No, Daddy, don't…"

Chapter Twenty

Sharon awakened to the sound of sirens. *What's going on? Never hear sirens in Burnsville. Boy what a headache. Need an aspirin.* She reached to turn on the bedside lamp.

"Lie still, please."

Opening her eyes, she became aware of her surroundings: the semi-hard surface of the gurney, the too-bright light inside the ambulance, the sensation of moving, the strange man sitting beside her, the blood-pressure cuff on her arm, the gizmo on the tip of her finger measuring her pulse and various vital signs.

"Who…" Her voice sounded raspy, she tried again. "Who are you?"

"David Baxter. EMT. There was an accident. We're taking you to the hospital. UAMS." He removed the stethoscope and loosened the BP cuff. Fishing a penlight from his breast pocket he shone it in her eyes. "Can you tell me your name?'

"Sharon. Sharon Jordan."

"Good. Your address?"

"I live in Burnsville. 135 Harbor."

"Who's the President of the United States."

"George Bush … why would you ask me that?"

"Do you know what happened to you tonight?"

"Oh … yes. We were at a party. Where's my mother?"

"She was a little upset. A friend's bringing her."

"She was having a fit, huh?"

David smiled. "Pretty much. They'll meet us there. Do you wear contacts?"

"Yes, I do. My mother … I'm her only child. All that energy comes my way."

"I guess the sight of blood scared her. May I remove your contacts? I need to take a look in your eyes."

"Sure." With effort, she widened her eyes. *Blood? Oh. No.* "Where's Mary Kay?"

"She must be in another unit. Do you know what day this is?"

"Stop that! Is she okay?"

"I'm sorry. I don't know her status."

The ambulance pulled into the emergency entrance at University of Arkansas for Medical Sciences where Sally waited at the door. Inside a cubicle, she and a nurse helped Sharon change into a hospital gown. The nurse put Sharon's clothes into a plastic bag. "The police may need these for evidence," she said. "At any rate, you won't want them back."

"Where did all that blood come from?" Sharon asked.

"Well, dear, that lady fell right on top of you," Sally said.

"Good grief! You mean Mary Kay? She bled all over me? Is she okay? What about Kris?"

"That awful man took her with him. I was in the kitchen and heard the gun … ruckus."

A gunshot. Kris' tiny, frightened voice. Sharon sat up in the bed. "Mother, I am fine. I don't need you holding my hand. Do you have my purse? I need my glasses and phone."

"I don't think you're supposed to use a cell phone in here."

"Mother, humor me, please. Go see if you can find out about Mary Kay."

A nurse appeared at the edge of the privacy curtain. "There's a police detective here who wants to talk to you. Are you up to it?"

"Sure. I have some questions for him, too."

"Mrs. Jordan, I'm Sgt. Lionel Higgins, Little Rock Police." He glanced at Sally.

"Hello," Sharon said, "This is my mother, Sally Seabring. Before I answer any of your questions, I want you to tell me what happened to Mary Kay and Kris."

"Mrs. Bonner ... died at the scene. The child was abducted by the perpetrator." He pulled out a notebook and pen. "Can you tell me what happened at the church tonight?"

Sharon lay back on the pillow. The detective's words confirmed the fear that had nagged at her consciousness. In halting phrases, she recounted the events of the evening.

"He knocked you out?"

"Well, I heard the shot."

"So, you didn't see the actual shooting?"

"No, my head was down."

"Well, thanks, Mrs. Jordan." He handed her a business card. "If you think of anything else, call me. When we catch this guy we may want you to come in and ID him."

"Okay. What about Kris?"

"There's a Morgan Nick Alert across Arkansas right now and an Amber Alert will go out after midnight. That covers all the states. We're hopeful he won't hurt his own daughter."

"He killed his wife!"

"Yes ma'am. Well, if you think of anything, give us a call."

The nurse poked her head around the curtain. "All finished here? You're scheduled for the lab and x-ray."

Chapter Twenty-One

At 6:00 am, Sharon sat in a wheelchair in the lobby of the hospital emergency room, release papers and prescription for pain medication lying in her lap. After hours of tests and observation, the diagnosis: a slight concussion. "Take it easy for a few days and see your family doctor in a week," the ER resident said.

Sally adjusted the blanket covering Sharon's legs. "I'll just run warm up the car. Do you know the temperature dropped to fifteen degrees last night? I hope your daddy left the water dripping in the downstairs bathroom. You'll need to put on your coat. That nice pastor Mr. Adams brought your things over a little while ago. Bless his heart, he's just devastated by all this."

"Mother, do you have my purse?"

"Yes, dear. What is it you want?"

Sharon retrieved her phone and billfold. She had never called the number scribbled on the back of Roger's business card. It lay in the slot with various other cards since the day he gave it to her at the Visitor Center in Nebraska. *Six o'clock. He's up.* She punched buttons. *Maybe on his way to work.*

"Johnson here."

"Roger…"

"…Sharon?"

She held the phone tight against her face, opened and closed her mouth. The tears for Mary Kay and Kris weighed heavy in her chest. She could not weep, she could not speak. She heard Roger's voice next to her cheek.

"Sharon? Is that you? Are you okay?"

Sally gently pried the instrument from the shaking fingers and spoke into it. "Roger? I'm Sally Seabring, Sharon's mother…" She walked a few feet away and continued to talk softly.

Sharon wiped her face on the sleeve of the hospital scrubs the nurse had given her. She took a deep breath, fighting for composure. Sally returned with the phone; Roger was still on the line.

"I'll be there as soon as I can."

"Oh, Roger. I know I should say don't bother to come so far, but I do want to talk to you."

"I know. Just let me rearrange some things here. Go home and get some rest. I'll call when I know my ETA."

***

In the dim light filtering through the bedroom windows, Sharon couldn't tell if she was waking to dawn or dusk. The clock beside her bed read 5:30. *Did Roger call?* Upon arriving home, she had fallen gratefully into bed and was asleep within minutes. She didn't protest when Sally removed the phone from the room. *Sometimes it feels good just to relax and let Mother take care of things.*

The pain in her head had settled to a dull ache. In the bathroom, she splashed water in her eyes and examined her face in the mirror. The lump on her head was receding and a dark blue splotch of skin surrounded the wound. The flesh below her eye was a purple bruise.

"Oh, honey, you're awake." Sally bustled into the bedroom. "I made some soup. You need to eat. Your daddy took his supper in the den to watch the news. Do you feel like joining him? I'll bring it to you."

Sharon curled up on the couch beside Earl just as the newsman began his opening remarks.

"Good Evening. Little Rock marked its 49th homicide of 2004 when violence erupted at a children's Christmas party. Ralph Bonner of North Little Rock …" He continued to recount the last night's events, as photos of Kris,

Mary Kay and her estranged husband flashed across the screen. Ralph Bonner's face, calm and smiling slightly, hardly resembled the deranged man who killed his wife and kidnapped his daughter in front of a room full of witnesses. According to the news report, the shooter's whereabouts were unknown. The authorities assumed Kris was with him.

Sally came in with a tray holding a bowl of steaming soup. "Here's your supper. That's enough news, Earl. Turn it off."

"Wait!" Sharon sat up as the TV anchorman began details of another story.

"The death of a homeless man yesterday evening was attributed to sub-freezing temperatures in the Little Rock area. Two transients who had spent the night in a shelter returned to their campsite this morning to discover the body of their friend. He was lying inside a refrigerator box covered with only an Army blanket. Just moments ago the man was identified as George Hunter, originally from Fort Smith. No other information is available at this time."

Sharon realized she stood in front of the television set. Words of denial poured from her. Tears that refused to fall earlier now flowed freely down her face.

"Sharon!" She turned to see Roger standing in the doorway. Seconds later she was enveloped in the warmth and safety of his arms.

"Oh, Roger," she said against his chest. "I prayed for them. God was supposed to keep them safe."

Chapter Twenty-Two

"I told my mom about the sweet tea here in Arkansas. She tried her hand at it, but it didn't taste the same." Roger set his glass down. Sally had cooked lunch while Earl and Roger ran errands. Now the four of them sat around the table in Sharon's dining room.

"The secret," Sally said, "is lots of sugar, added while the tea is hot."

"That's right," Sharon put in. "About a cup of sugar. Everything else is just 'sweetened' tea, not Sweet Tea."

"I don't know how you all can drink that stuff when it's twenty degrees outside. You people are freezing me to death." Earl pushed back from the table. "Good lunch, Mother."

Roger nodded. "Yes, indeed, Mrs. Seabring. It was delicious. I'm sorry to have to leave so soon, but I need to start back."

"We're sorry, too, but we understand. And call me 'Sally.'" She gathered a stack of dishes and moved toward the kitchen, stopping at the door. "Why don't you help me in here, Earl."

He stood obediently. "That means I'm supposed to clear out and let you two talk in private. Good to meet you, Roger. Have a safe trip home."

Sharon walked into the den and Roger followed.

"Nice folks," he said.

"Thanks. They like you, too. Where did you and Daddy run off to this morning?"

"Oh, we stopped at the hardware store and then drove out to check on things at the farm."

Sharon smiled. "Guy stuff, huh?"

"Yeah, it was fun." He took her hand and they sat on the couch. "Feeling better?"

"I slept well. The pain pills helped, I'm sure. I can't seem to slow my mind enough to relax. Too many questions."

"Well, I got a few answers for you this morning. Last October at the seminar I met a guy who works for the Arkansas state police. He did me a favor and asked around about this case. Ralph Bonner is a store manager at Skate Board City, in the mall in North Little Rock. All the folks there consider him an upstanding guy. But at home, apparently it's a different story. His neighbors called the police a couple of times last year. Once because of yelling and screaming coming from the house and once because the little girl ran next door saying 'Daddy's hurting Mommy.'"

"Ohhh, Kris. Bless her heart."

"Both times, Mary Kay backed out of pressing charges. One day a couple of months ago he came home from work and she and Kris were gone. He didn't know it then, but they were at the shelter. Her parents, Mr. and Mrs. Kopel, live in Yellville and are coming to claim the body. The Kopels want custody of the little girl when she's found. The family's been estranged because Mary Kay wouldn't press charges. She told them she was afraid of him. Now they know why.

"The state police are watching all of Bonner's known relatives in case he tries to hide the girl. The FBI can track him through his social security number if he settles in another state and gets a job. They'll watch his credit cards. Unless he had a bunch of money in his pocket, he may be in trouble."

"Thank you, Roger. Do you think there's a chance they'll find him?"

"Maybe. I doubt he had planned where to go and what to do. Seems like he acted from anger, not premeditation. And about George..."

"Yes?"

"We have no way of knowing if George Hunter is the same man you met at the free lunch. His family came from Fort Smith to claim his body. While he was on drugs, he stole from them several times and they cut him off. But he was their son and they loved him. They're hurting. I don't want to sound trite, but … seriously … he's in a better place."

Roger touched Sharon's bruised face with the tips of his fingers. "My brave girl. Give it some time. The questions, like this tender spot, will clear up."

She knew he wasn't talking about George any more. "I guess so. I sure don't understand why this had to happen. All things about God are such a mystery. At one time I wouldn't even discuss them. When Tim tried to start a serious conversation, I would make a joke and change the subject. But since Tim died, I've come to realize how important his faith was to him. I'm curious about how that works. I thought if I asked, God would take care of people who mean something to me. I've worked so hard … going to church, helping out, trying to do the right thing…"

"Sharon, you think if you're a good little girl, tithe and say your prayers God is going to do everything your way? That's not faith. That's a business deal. Quid pro quo. God gives us free will. George was anti-social. He made the decision to stay in a box instead of taking shelter. That was his choice and it was a bad one."

"I can see what you mean, but it makes me wonder why anyone would bother to pray if someone's free will is what controls the situation…"

"Ralph Bonner is a sinner, a wife beater and now a murderer. God gave him free will, too, and he misused it. Mary Kay was the victim."

"Was it that God *couldn't* protect her or that he chose not to?"

"That's a hard question I don't know if I have an answer for. I just believe she's with God right now and He's taking care of her." He turned her hand over, kissed the palm. "I believe God took care of you. Every mile I drove from Nebraska to Arkansas, I thanked God for your safety."

His lips brushed hers lightly and he held her for a moment. "Gotta go," he whispered in her ear. "I hope we can still do New Year's weekend."

"Thank you for coming. Let me think about New Year's…"

He stepped back and looked into her eyes. "I'll call you tomorrow."

Sharon stood at the door until his car pulled away, then walked into the kitchen as Sally finished loading the dishwasher.

"Did Roger leave?" she asked.

"Yes. Where's Daddy?"

"He's changing your furnace filters."

"Daddy doesn't need to do that!"

"Let him do it for you. That's how men are. Often, they don't know how to take care of women, so they fix your car or things around the house. If it wasn't so cold, he'd probably be changing the oil in your car."

"I never thought of that."

Sally shut the dishwasher and pushed the button. "When we were first married, your dad would get so angry when I cried. He thought I was manipulating him. I cried so easily. Finally, one day I told him, 'It's got nothing to do with you. You don't have to do anything when I cry. But if you want to hold me, it would help.' And that's what he does. For over forty years, when I cry he keeps his mouth shut and holds me."

"That's a great story, Mother."

"I think Roger knows what to do when a woman cries."

Sharon smiled. "I guess he does. It seems foolish now that I needed him to drive 500 miles just to give me a hug."

"Not foolish at all."

CHAPTER TWENTY-THREE

About noon on December 23 it began to snow. Earl announced he needed to go to the farm and insisted Sally and Sharon go along. "We're supposed to get three or four inches and if we're gonna get snowed in, we need to be at home."

The storm continued all day, then the temperature dropped, creating a crust of ice on top of the snow. Central Arkansas looked like a Christmas card scene; traffic came to a halt. Christmas Eve services were cancelled and the Little Rock airport shut down.

Sharon commented little on any of these happenings. At the farm, she spent her time shut up in her old bedroom or on the living room couch, remote in hand, staring at the television set while she moved aimlessly through the channels.

On December 26, two events took place. On an international scale, a tsunami hit Thailand and several Asian countries killing thousands; and, in Oklahoma, Ralph Bonner was arrested in a Tulsa hospital where he had sought medical help. The next day, Roger called.

"Hi, Sharon. I guess you heard they caught Bonner."

"Yes, some detective called me."

"It was one of those fluke things. Did he tell you how it happened?"

"No, just that it was in a hospital in Tulsa."

"Well, it seems when Bonner hit Mary Kay across the face, he broke her tooth and scratched his hand on the jagged edge. We call it a fight bite. Anyway, this injury on his hand got inflamed. Human bites can set up a real bad infection. Are you with me so far?"

"Yes."

"A couple of days after he took off with Kris, Bonner's hand swells up. So, he puts some antibiotic cream on it. Then it gets really sore and he's spiking a temperature of 103. He goes to one of those walk-in clinics in Tulsa and passes out before he sees a doctor. Kris is sitting there in the waiting room. They call 911 for him and the Department of Human Services to see about the little girl. He had given them a phony name and a lame story about how he got the injury. So, at the hospital, they called the police and started checking things out and found the Amber Alert and the Arkansas warrants on him. That's great, huh?"

"Great?"

"I just love the irony ... that Mary Kay nabbed her own killer."

"I guess so."

"Sharon? Are you okay?"

"I'm fine."

"Did the detective want you to come down and identify Bonner?"

"I don't think I can do that."

"What?" Silence for several seconds. "Well, you can decide later. After the weather clears. They have plenty to hold him on for now."

"The weather has nothing to do with it. I'm not going to be in the same room with that man. No one can make me."

"You won't be in the same room. It's behind a two-way mirror..."

"Roger, leave me alone about this."

"Okay, okay. Later."

"No, not later."

Again there was silence across the miles. Finally, Roger spoke. "Do you think the airport will be open by the 30th? We're still on for New Year's Eve, aren't we?"

"No, I don't think that will be possible."

"Really? The weather bureau…"

"I'm not talking about the weather, Roger."

"You're not coming?"

"Stop pressuring me!" Sharon's voice became shrill.

"Now listen, Sharon…" She could hear anger, heard him take a deep breath. "Okay, sorry. I don't think I've applied any pressure. Actually, I believe originally the idea was yours."

"Maybe so. But that's over. There's no point in us seeing each other again. I'll never marry you. I would be a horrible wife for you. I can't … I can't do that."

"Wait, this is something we can talk about."

"No! We're not going to talk about it! I'm not going to… You would resent me, maybe even hate me. No. We stop this before we fall in love."

"Too late for that."

"I'm sorry, Roger. It's not going to happen. We need to end it. Don't call me any more."

The silence was so long this time, Sharon thought he had hung up. When he spoke again, his voice was calm.

"Sharon, I told you the first … well the second time we met that I want to be your friend. That's still true. I won't call you if you don't want me to but I'd still like to email you. I like talking to you. I want to tell you about Todd's Christmas program. It was hilarious. We can talk about whatever you want to. I'll back off. But we're still friends. Okay?"

Without answering, Sharon put down the phone, breaking the connection.

CHAPTER TWENTY-FOUR

Sharon lay on the daybed in her old room at the farm and gazed at the family pictures that lined the wall. The room that once housed a child, a teen and finally a young woman home from college had changed gradually over the years. Currently used for Sally's sewing projects, the room had become a sanctuary for Sharon.

A knock on the door interrupted her reverie. "Telephone," Sally said. "It's Eve." After a moment, Sharon stuck out her hand, took the phone and closed the door.

"Hello."

"Sharon! Oh my gosh, are you okay?"

"Define 'okay.'"

"Yeah, really! I called to tell you 'Happy New Year' and your mom answered your cell."

"Yes. I'm at my parents' house."

"She told me everything that happened. I thought you'd be out somewhere with Roger. You didn't come to Nebraska?"

"No. It didn't seem like the thing to do."

"Oh, Sharon, I'm so sorry. So what happens now? Will you be coming later?"

Sharon was silent for a time. "Eve, I know this … this thing with Roger caught your romantic fancy, but it's not going to happen."

"Wait a minute. I'll admit I thought it was … oh, tender, poetic … the way you two met and all, but I also felt it might be God's plan for you. You both seem to want the same things."

Sharon didn't respond, so Eve went on. "Take it from me, you're going to need to talk to someone about the bad things you saw. About how you feel."

"I don't think so. I just need to forget it. Put it out of my mind."

"Oh, Sharon, seriously now… Well, if you change your mind and want to talk, I'm here."

"Thanks, Eve. You're a friend."

"I'll call again in a few days and see how you are."

"Thanks, but I'll be fine."

***

"Oh, there you are, Honey. Still in your pajamas?" Sally set her cup of coffee on the end table and picked up her knitting. "No mail today. Martin Luther King's birthday. Banks are closed too, but Earl still found a reason to go to town."

Sharon pointed the remote control at the TV and punched buttons.

"I thought you were going to work today," Sally said.

"No. Daddy's going to stop by my house and pick up my laptop so I can send them a file. I don't feel like going anywhere."

"Oh."

Sharon muted the sound and turned to her mother. "I may quit that job."

"Quit your job? What would you do all day?"

"I don't know. But when I think of going back to that office I can't stand it." Her voice quivered and her eyes filled.

"All right, Honey. We can talk about it later."

Sharon turned back to the television and Sally knitted in silence. The younger woman flipped through the channels, watching a program only minutes before moving on to something new. After awhile, Sally lay her knitting aside and left the room.

Shortly before noon Earl returned with the laptop computer and lay it on the coffee table in front of Sharon. She pulled her gaze away from *Dialing for Dollars* and looked up at him.

"Thanks, Daddy."

"Still in your pj's?"

Before Sharon answered, Sally came bustling into the room. "You're back. My goodness you were gone all morning. We were wondering about you. I made some tuna salad. I thought we'd have sandwiches for lunch. I'll have it on the table in just a minute…"

"Never mind." Earl switched off the TV and sank into the arm chair across from Sharon. "Sit down, Sally."

She lowered herself into a chair and said, "What is it, Earl?"

"After I picked up the computer, I went by the church to see Jerry Thompson."

"Well, that was nice…" Sally murmured. Sharon raised her head.

"I wanted to talk to him about you, Sharon."

"Me?"

"Yes. Your mother and I are worried about you and I needed to talk to someone about it."

"Daddy, there's nothing wrong with me. Why would you want to bring a stranger into something that's my concern?"

"First of all, he's not a stranger. He's your pastor. And second, there *is* something wrong with you. Here it is twelve noon and you're still in your sleepers, you don't want to go to your own home, you won't go to work, you cry if anyone says boo to you…"

"Earl," Sally said. "She's not feeling well. This isn't the time."

"It is time. It's the middle of January, the snow has melted, she has a home, she has a job and responsibilities."

Sharon stood. "I'm right here. I can hear you. If you don't want me around, I'll leave…" Her voice broke as she plopped onto the couch and buried her face in her hands.

Earl's voice softened. "Look, Honey, I talked to Brother Thompson. He knows about things like this. He says you've been through a lot lately. You witnessed a violent crime. You were a victim yourself. Just because the bruise on your face is fading, there's still a big hurt inside you that hasn't healed. He called it…" He pulled a note from his pocket. "…post traumatic stress disorder."

"What is that?" Sally asked.

"When something bad happens to someone, or maybe even if they just see something … uh … traumatic, it jars their nervous system and they might have a hard time snapping out of it. They came up with this term when the Viet Nam vets were having emotional problems. It's like…"

"There's nothing wrong with Sharon's mind."

Sharon looked at both her parents. "Never mind, Mother. I've heard of it, Daddy. I know what you're talking about."

"So, what are the symptoms?" Sally said.

Earl referred to his note. "Hard time sleeping, overly emotional, lack of concentration, unmotivated, unrealistic fears…" He looked at Sally. "Sound familiar?"

"Daddy," Sharon spoke up, "I don't know why you're pushing me. I'm just tired. I need a little time…"

"Sharon … Honey. Your mother and I love you more than anything. She'd let you stay here forever, taking care of you while you prowl the house all night and sleep all day. But, my love for you is going to take a different path. You need to talk to someone about this. Maybe you want to meet with Jerry Thompson."

"I certainly do not. He told me I need to forgive the little snot that killed Tim!"

"Well, you're going to have to do something to get yourself together." He threw three business cards on the table. "Here's the names of some counselors your preacher recommended. Choose one. Make an appointment. Make an effort to help yourself."

Sharon picked up the cards and read the names: Lloyd Grant, PhD; Patricia Norman, LCSW; Stephen Cooper, MSW.

"I guess I could talk to Patti...."

Chapter Twenty-Five

Earl pulled his pickup into a space in the Walmart parking lot. Sharon, in the passenger seat, gazed out the window.

"I'll just wait here in the car," she said.

"No you won't. The purpose of this trip is to get you out of the house. You didn't call that counselor. You say you can do it on your own. Now, get out of this truck. We're going to Walmart." Earl walked around the front of the vehicle and opened the passenger door.

Sighing heavily, Sharon swung her legs around, slid out of the truck and stood beside him.

"Daddy, I don't know why you're being so bossy." She tried to smile, make a joke as she took her dad's arm and they made their way inside. Saturday morning and the discount store's aisles were packed. *Why am I afraid to go shopping?*

"I'm looking for a new cap," Earl said, heading toward the back of the store. "You coming?"

"No, I … I'll just look around up here. Maybe I'll find a movie. I'll be near the check out when you finish." She studied the display of DVD's, then moved to a rack of magazines, raising her head periodically to glance around. *I wish Daddy would hurry. How long can it take to get a camouflage hat just like the one he buys every year?*

"Hey, I'm back. Did you find anything?" Sharon spun around. Earl touched her arm and she followed him to the checkout line. A man with a child moved in behind them. The small girl sitting in the basket reached out and grabbed a candy bar from the display. The man retrieved the sweet and returned it. The little girl's face clouded up, she stretched toward the candy and whined, "No, Daddy, don't..."

The tiny voice pierced Sharon. She put her hand to her temple as she felt again the blow of the gun against her head. She fell on all fours, the weight of Mary Kay's body pushing her down and the sound of the gunshot ringing in her ears.

"Noooo," she screamed. "Stop it, stop it." She sank the rest of the way to the floor and lay sobbing, her breath coming in short gasps. Earl whirled around to see Sharon lying in a heap, wedged between shopping baskets and checkout lanes. The man yanked the child from the cart and took several steps backward.

"Ma'am, are you all right?" The Walmart checker came from behind his counter. He spoke to Earl, "Is she with you? Is she all right?"

Earl stood helplessly. "Yes, she's my daughter. I don't know..." He bent over Sharon. "Honey, what's wrong? What upset you?" He stroked her shoulder and Sharon screamed.

"Stop him! He shot Mary Kay. Don't let him take Kris."

A store manager alerted by an associate hurried to the aisle where Sharon lay. "Excuse me. I think I know what's happening." He knelt beside Sharon and spoke to Earl. "She may be having a flashback ... reliving something bad that happened. Could that be it?"

Earl nodded.

"What's her name?"

"Sharon."

The young man touched Sharon's arm. She recoiled.

"Ma'am ... Sharon. Listen to me. You're safe. You're here in Walmart."

A moan came from the heap on the floor.

"Listen. You can hear me. My name's Wayne. Can you feel my hand on your arm?"

An imperceptible nod.

"I know it's scary. But you're safe. You're in Burnsville, Arkansas. In Walmart. Hear the cash registers? Feel the smooth tile you're lying on? Open your eyes and see where you are"

As he spoke, Sharon's breathing returned to near normal. Head still down, she peered at the vinyl beneath her.

"Good. You can see and feel the floor. It's real. The scary things you hear aren't real. Can you look at me?"

She rolled to her side and looked up at the manager and Earl, her face ashen underneath tear-stained blotches.

"Hi, Daddy. What happened?"

Wayne Kensett and Earl gave Sharon a hand up off the floor. They walked to the manager's office in the customer service area of the store. Trembling, Sharon sank into a chair.

"I …" Earl began, cleared his throat. "I don't know how to thank you, Wayne."

"That's okay. I think it was a flashback. They're pretty terrifying for the person having one, and for the people watching. She was totally reliving an event that felt dangerous. The best thing to do is remind her of where she is and that she's safe."

"How did you know that?"

"Oh …" He shrugged. "I'm a vet … seen this before. So what happened to her?"

"She saw a murder."

"Yeah, that would do it okay. Does she have a counselor?"

"Not yet. But she's gonna." Earl said with finality.

CHAPTER TWENTY-SIX

Session One: January 24, 2005

The following Tuesday, Sharon allowed Sally to drive her to Patti Norman's office in Woodbine. They sat in the waiting room without speaking. Patti entered from an inside door.

"Hello, Sharon. How are you?"

"She's a little shaky," Sally volunteered.

"Never mind, Mother. Hello, Patti. I'm okay."

"Well, come in. Would you like some coffee?" Leaving Sally in the waiting room, they settled in plush chairs in Patti's office.

"Tell me why you're here," Patti said.

"My dad insisted."

"Tell me why."

Sharon related the details of the incident at the children's Christmas party in Little Rock while Patti listened, occasionally making a note. When Sharon paused, Patti said, "I'm sorry this happened to you, but it's good you can talk about it. Can you tell me how you were feeling while all this was taking place?"

"When I was moving toward him, asking him to let Kris go, I felt scared, but confident. Strong. I really thought he was going to do it. Then he'd go away and it would all be over. Later, in the ambulance … and at the hospital … as it dawned on me … what … had … happened to Mary Kay …" She buried her face in her hands. Patti waited silently for Sharon to continue.

"Part of me refused to believe it, even when the police officer told me. And he said it like, 'Oh, she died.' Like he might say, 'It's Tuesday.' So matter of fact. I wanted to hit him."

She dried her face with a handful of tissues and gave Patti a wry smile. "But I was sitting on a gurney in a cubicle in the ER, wearing only a hospital gown. Any sudden action would definitely have exposed my backside."

Patti leaned back in her chair. "Some sense of humor still in there? That's good."

"Really? Not disrespectful? Most of the time I feel I should never laugh or even smile again because Tim's gone and Mary Kay's dead. We were friends. And Kris. She's lost her mother. Her daddy, too, such as he was. I'm a grown-up and I'm a basket case. What must it be like for a child? I have no way of knowing if she's okay..." Sharon again dissolved into tears, saying between sobs, "I'm sorry."

"It's okay to cry. Pretty understandable, I would say."

"All this has made me ... nervous. I ... just ... want some time to recoup. But my parents think what I need is help ... someone to talk to."

"What do you think?"

Sharon dried her face once more. "Maybe."

"How are you sleeping?"

"Not so well. The pain pills help."

"Are you having pain?"

"No. I did. And the ER doctor gave me the pills. I take one when I can't sleep."

"I'm sure he also told you to follow up with your family doctor. Have you done that?"

"No. Not yet."

"Sharon. I'd like for us to agree on a contract. You come talk to me once a week for six weeks. Will you do that?"

"I guess so."

"I'm going to take that as a 'yes.' Also, see your doctor for that follow up visit. He needs to know what's going on with you. If you sign a release, I can talk to him, too. Up to you."

"Okay."

"And, let's try some other things to help you sleep. Save the pain killers for pain. We don't want you to get dependent on them. If you need medication for sleep, I can suggest that to your doctor. But first, let's try this…" Sharon read the 3x5 card Patti handed to her.

No caffeine after 3:00 p.m.
No afternoon naps.
Exercise during the day.
Warm baths before bedtime (bubbles are good).
Soothing music in the bedroom.
No mystery stories before bedtime – inspirational or devotional reading is good.

Patti filled out an appointment card. "Sharon, you witnessed a terrible act. I don't want you to push it from your memory, but just for this next week, when it comes to mind, don't dwell on it. If there's anything particular you want us to talk about, make a note. Journaling is good. Have you had a flashback?"

"I think so."

"Tell me about it."

"I sort of weirded out. Right there in Walmart. I heard something that sounded like Kris. It felt like…" Sharon paused, groped for a word to describe the incident.

"Like it was happening all over again?" Patti interrupted. "A flashback is not like a dream or a memory or thought. It's when you relive the experience in such a realistic manner that you have the same physical and emotional reactions you had during the original experience. It can be triggered by something as innocent as an odor or sound."

"I guess that's what happened."

"It can be frightening. If it happens again, call me. If I'm not in, my voice mail will link you to the Crisis Center where someone can talk you through it."

"Okay."

"I'm glad you're here, Sharon. I'll see you next week."

Chapter Twenty-Seven

Session Two: January 31, 2005

"Hi, Sharon. How are you today?"

"I'm okay."

"Good. Sleeping better?"

"Yes. Your suggestions work."

"Good. Is there something specific you want to talk about today?"

"I don't know. I told you everything last week."

"I see. So, do you feel able to move back home? Go back to work?"

"I just need some time …"

"Okay. Since we agreed to meet for six weeks, let's get started. Tell me about Mary Kay."

"Mary Kay? She was my friend. On the surface it would seem we had nothing in common, but there was a connection there. Hard to explain."

"Try."

"She was so brave. I knew she must be worried and tense, living in hiding like she was, but sometimes she seemed to be able to put the tension aside. Then, she'd laugh and play with Kris … using a squeaky voice with the hand puppets or letting Kris win at Shoots and Ladders. Her death was a personal loss for me." Sharon looked away from Patti, out the window, at the winter day. "Just add it to the list."

"List?"

"All the people … and things … that have been taken away from me."

"What else is on your list?"

"Well … Tim, of course. And our child … or the child that might have been ours."

"Go on."

"Mary Kay … and Kris … and … and George."

Patti looked up. "I don't know who George is. Tell me about him."

"Well, that's the crazy thing. I met him only once. I didn't really know him. His name was George Hunter." Sharon told about her meeting with the homeless man. "Then he died the same night Mary Kay did. He froze to death."

"And you feel his death is a personal loss?"

"Yes. Yes, I do. Personal."

"Why do you think that's so?"

"I don't know. Maybe because in a different way, we connected, too. With one look he saw through me. I had told myself I was doing something worthwhile, pouring tea for the less fortunate. And he zapped me with his honesty. So, I decided to pray for him to see if it would help him. Apparently it didn't."

"What did you lose when George died?"

"Oh, maybe the chance to…. I wanted to help him and didn't know how."

"If you could let George know something … anything … right now, what would that be?"

"That I really did care."

Chapter Twenty-Eight

Session Three: February 7, 2005

"Come in, Sharon. Did you cut your hair?"

"Yes. I ... I'm thinking about going back to work tomorrow."

"Good for you. How's that working out?"

"Well, they've been pretty nice about letting me work on the computer at home. I guess it's time to go back."

"Are you still staying at the farm?"

"No, I moved back home Wednesday. After our session."

"Good for you." Patti settled in her chair. "Last week we talked about your losses. Can you think of anything you gained this year that might balance things out a bit?"

Sharon thought a moment. "I've met some people, made some friends. Folks in the support group ... Eve and her family. They're really great people and such an inspiration on how to overcome.... You know, it's strange, I was about to say I've become more mature, more self-sufficient since Tim died. But on the other hand, Ralph Bonner pulls a trigger and I completely lose control of my life and end up in a weepy heap in my parents' house. That was a loss."

"Do you feel that moving back home and returning to work will help you regain control?"

"Yes, I guess I do. But, it's ironic how gains and losses move back and forth from one list to the other."

"Oh?"

"Yes. A dear friend … and the hope for love and companionship … was a gain this year. But now, because I'm weak, that relationship has to be listed in the lost column."

"You're weak?

"Yes. He's … great and I would still like to have him as a friend, someone to talk to. Someone to lean on. But that seems so selfish when he clearly wants our relationship to be more than that. It was the only fair thing. To cut him loose."

Patti filled two cups from the carafe. Handing one to Sharon, she said, "Tell me."

"His name is Roger. He works for the Nebraska State Police, in the traffic division. I met him after Tim's death." Sharon pulled a throw pillow onto her lap, traced the fabric design with her finger. "I was angry and he became the focus of my anger. But he was patient and sincerely friendly. Then, at Thanksgiving out of nowhere, he asked me to marry him.

"Oh?"

"I had never seen him that way, but I agreed to keep an open mind as we got to know each other better. Of course, I had a very selfish reason for going forward … the possibility of having a child one day."

"Not the best reason to get married."

"I suppose not. Then this thing … this murder … happened to change everything."

"How does this change things?"

"I can't take a chance on losing anyone else. Roger's a policeman. Something could happen to him."

"Didn't you say he's in the traffic division?"

"Yes, but that can be dangerous, too. Haven't you heard of officers getting killed making a routine traffic stop? Or being hit by a passing car while writing a ticket?" Sharon hugged the pillow to her chest. "Do we have to talk about this today?"

"No. Not at all. I can see you feel vulnerable. We can table this for awhile. But one day we'll need to talk about hard things. For now, I'd like for you to journal this week about how you feel. Begin each entry with 'today I feel…', then explore those emotions that come up. And remember we're dealing with feelings, not head trips."

"Head trips?"

"People say, 'I feel like a trip to the mall. I feel like that's a good movie.' Those are opinions, not feelings. We say, 'I feel thirsty or tired.' That's our brain telling us we need to rest or hydrate. I want you to identify that you feel happy, sad, afraid, frustrated, angry. Then write about why you feel that way."

Chapter Twenty-Nine

Session Four: February 14, 2005

"Sharon, can we talk about Ralph Bonner today?"

"I'm not ready for that. It's Valentine's Day. Can't we talk about happy things?" When Patti didn't answer, Sharon continued, "I can't go point him out, if that's what you mean."

"Can we explore why you think you can't do that?"

"Don't you see? He's responsible for half the losses on my list."

"How do you mean he's responsible?"

"Before that nightmare, I felt safe in my world ... and in control of my life. When I stopped feeling secure, I lost control of where I went and what I did. Did you know there was a time I felt safe enough to go look for George in homeless camps?"

"Might that have also been naïve of you?"

"Okay, then. I've lost my naïveté, too. I thought if I spoke kindly and calmly I could talk that monster out of leaving with Kris. What did I get for my trouble? He cracked me upside the head and shot Mary Kay." Sharon reached for a tissue on the end table. "Kris must really be afraid now. Seeing her mother shot, then her daddy grabbing her up like that and taking her off ... and the whole deal in Oklahoma ... police and social workers and foster care..."

"Do you know where she is now?"

"No. I heard that her grandparents want her, but I don't know..."

"Why do you suppose you feel such an attachment to Kris?"

"I don't know. She caught my attention when she and her mother came to the free lunch. I thought they were homeless, then found out later they were in Safe House. Maybe I attached to Kris because I had so recently dealt with the hopelessness of ever having a child of my own."

'That's good. Go on."

"Mary Kay wasn't the kind of friend you go to the mall with, but the sort you can trust ... open up to. I didn't, but I could have. I never knew anyone in her situation ... at least I don't think so. Then I learned of the sheer terror she lived with. He said he would kill her. He almost did once, and she fully believed that one day it would happen. And she was right. He won."

"Are you afraid he might hurt you?"

"I've been assured he can't. Not while he's locked up, anyway."

"Sharon if you decide that there is something you are able to do to insure he stays in jail, there would be some healing in it for you."

"Really?"

"Yes. When you're ready to do that, it would be saying to him, 'I'm in control, not you.'"

"Really?"

"Really. Think about it." They sat without speaking for a few minutes before Patti broke the silence. "Last week I asked you to journal about any feelings that might come up. Did you do that?"

"Yes, I did. It was interesting."

"What did you find out?"

"Well, one night I woke up terrified and I didn't know why. I'm not nervous or afraid to stay alone in my house ... that wasn't it. I couldn't imagine what had hold of me. I began to write and try to remember what I had been dreaming about just before I woke up."

"Could you remember?"

"Finally, it came to me. In my dream I was completely isolated in the world. As a result of a disaster I was the only person left alive on earth. I wandered around looking for another human being but there was no one. The more I searched the more frightened I became."

"Did you decide what this might mean?"

"I have never been afraid of solitude. I'm a private person. I need time to myself to re-energize. But this was different. This was total aloneness with no hope of ever seeing another person. That was frightening. I don't want to live like that."

"You don't want to live alone?"

"I don't want to live without hope."

Chapter Thirty

Session Five: February 21, 2005

"Patti, I've come to a conclusion."

"Hello, Sharon, come in. Tell me about your conclusion."

"I'm a very selfish person."

"I'm not sure I follow..."

"My whole life has been about me."

"Do you want to explain that?"

"Most everything in life has gone my way. My parents gave me whatever I asked for. Tim usually did what I wanted. Roger would have made concessions. Like as not he would have given up a career that's important to him. But I wouldn't go there. I guess that's one act of decency in my favor."

"If you'll stop beating yourself up for a minute, I'd like clarification on some of this."

"Okay..."

"Now, about your parents. How is that relationship?"

"Good, I think. Mother tends to be a bit over-protective, but not over-bearing. Usually I can just remind her I'm not a ten-year-old and then we laugh it off. Daddy's a sweety. And wise. Doesn't say much, but when he does, everyone listens."

"And they gave you everything? Spoiled you?"

"Just about."

"Spring break in Florida when you were in high school? Things like that?"

"No, of course not. I knew better than to ask. I just mean ... well ... you know ... only child sort of stuff."

"You wanted something, they thought it was reasonable, they could afford it, so they agreed. Does that describe your childhood?"

"Yes, I guess so."

"Did you … do you feel they love you?"

"Heavens, yes!"

"And Tim?"

"Love me? Yes, of course. When he got out of the Navy, we had to decide where to live. I wanted to come to Arkansas and he said 'Okay.' I was the one who fell in love with the house we bought. And … and … I was the one who suggested it was time to start a family. It was my idea … he was reluctant …"

"He had issues to deal with. Do you think he compromised his values for you?"

"No, I would never have asked him to do that."

"Sharon, you said you ended a friendship with Roger because you were weak. Do you still feel that way?"

"I couldn't … I can't put myself in a situation where I might lose someone. I … I'm not strong enough to do that again. I just can't. His duties aren't extremely dangerous, but still … the potential is there. I was afraid if I had told him that…. I couldn't let him even think about giving up his career for me. So we didn't talk about it … or anything else…"

"When was this?"

"A couple of weeks before I came to see you."

"You haven't talked to him since?"

"No. He's emailed me but I haven't answered."

"Why?"

"I told you. I'm a selfish person. Every time Roger and I have been together it's because I needed help or someone to lean on. These things are supposed to be give and take. I never seem to give … just take-take-take." Sharon paused, took a deep breath.

"Sharon, I don't experience you as a self-centered person. I understand that up until the past year, your life has been relatively free of challenges. But that was just lucky for you, not of your doing. If your parents were willing to give you things they could afford, things that were reasonable, that's understandable. I'm sure if you had fallen on the floor in a tantrum, that would have been a different matter for them."

Sharon smiled. "You're right about that."

"You and Tim seemed to have a good relationship. Again, if you had made unrealistic demands on him he probably would have stood up to you. The fact that you two agreed on most things doesn't make either of you selfish. From what I know of you, you're generous and caring. You seem to realize your life has been blessed. I've seen you look for ways to give back."

Patti continued, "But if you feel led to, it never hurts to take an aggressive step toward being more sensitive to others. It's never wrong to try to see another perspective. It's often helpful. This event happened to you, but a lot of people saw it and they were affected, too. For instance, your mother …?"

"She was in the kitchen. She heard the commotion and came out to see Mary Kay and me sprawled in the floor, blood all over the place."

"So, how's she doing?"

"Wanting to shield me. Perfectly happy for me to be in my old room. Not too eager for me to move back to my house. I never thought about why she had become so clingy until now."

"And the children?"

"Most were at the other end of the hall by the Christmas tree. They were herded into the next room as quickly as possible. The pastor called in counselors to talk to them.

"…and the pastor … the church members?"

"I heard some of the members want to stop the ministry to the homeless … maybe relocate the congregation to a safer neighborhood."

"…and the hungry people who come each Sunday?"

"Gosh, that violence touched a lot of lives, didn't it?"

"It did. I'll see you next week."

Chapter Thirty-One

Session Six: February 28, 2005

"This is our last session, Sharon. Are you ready?"

"Yes, I think so."

"You can call me anytime you need to. Or call the crisis line. Those counselors are there for emotional support as well as crises. The anniversary of Tim's death is in a couple of weeks, isn't it? It's not unusual for there to be sadness around an anniversary. I think you're ready to use your own resources, but feel free to call if you need to." Patti picked up her pen and note pad. "Now. Can you tell me any decisions you've made as a result of our visits?"

"I've talked to the District Attorney in Little Rock. I'll testify in Ralph Bonner's trial when it comes up."

"Do you feel comfortable with that?"

"I'm okay. A little nervous, but I made up my mind myself. Nobody pushed me."

"Good. Anything else?"

"I've decided to change jobs."

"Well. This is new."

"I like the artistic challenge at Graphic Design and they've been good to me during this time. It's a pleasant atmosphere. But I want a job that's more people-oriented. Something that's more important than which shoes or deodorant someone chooses."

"I can understand that."

"A few weeks ago my boss gave me an assignment on some pro bono work the agency is doing. We're designing a logo for the Woodbine Literacy Council. They promote adult reading programs and train volunteers as tutors."

"Yes, I know."

"Before I started the actual design, I talked to the director, visited the center and watched some of the tutoring sessions. It was so inspiring, what they're able to accomplish. And I saw those people who work there, feeling so good that they spend their working day in worthwhile projects that help others. I have to make a living, but I would love for my work to make a difference. I think I'll explore the non-profit sector to see if there's a need for my skills. If I only knew..."

What?

"I was told God has a plan for my life, and I try to believe that. But I can't figure out what it is. I don't know what God wants from me."

"You don't?"

"Do you?"

"Well, I believe I know what God wants of *me.*"

"So how do I find out?"

"Sharon, I'm not trying to be mysterious, it's just that each person's experience is different. I see you working very hard, looking for God."

"Yes, I have. For the past several months. I'm not very patient."

"I don't think we find God by running around doing 'good works'. He comes into our lives and then we respond to that goodness. God's will ... His plan ... is for each one to have a relationship with Him. I don't know the Bible very well, but I know that somewhere there's a verse, 'If you seek, you will find.' Well ... something like that."

Sharon thought for a moment, then said, "There's a really beautiful anthem that goes, 'If with all your heart you truly seek me, You shall ever surely find me.'"

"Yes. That's a verse from the Bible." Patti thought for a moment. "And another says, 'Seek first the Kingdom of God and all these other things will be added.' God has to come first, then everything else follows. Jesus used the example of a plant … a vine. He's the vine and we're the branches. We have to be connected to him." She reached across the space between them and touched Sharon's hand.

"Sharon, I don't think there's ever a time when a light comes on in our heads, we snap our fingers and say, 'Aha! I know God's plan!' Because God's plan is too big for us to even imagine. Because it uses our lives and gifts and talents and meshes our gifts with everything that other people in the world have to give. Even though we don't completely understand, we just do the best we can. I believe that because you want it, God will send an answer."

Neither woman spoke for a time, then Patti brought out a colorful medium-sized box with a slit in the top. She set it on the table next to a stack of 3x5 cards.

"This is the worry box. Some call it the 'God box'. The premise is that you can write on a card anything you want to get rid of …worries, problems, or any situation you have no control over. When you drop it in the box, it's a symbolic way of giving it to God. He has it and there's no need for you to worry about it any more. Can you think of anything you might want to put in here?"

"Well … I guess I could put in Kris' welfare. I worry about it a lot, but there's really nothing I can do about it. Is that what you mean?"

"That's an excellent example." Patti waited while Sharon wrote on a card and slipped it through the slot. The two sat in silence for a time before Sharon spoke again.

"I've spent a lot of energy resenting that college student who killed Tim. It doesn't get me anywhere. I guess I should give it up."

"That's good." Patti stood. "Listen, you don't have to tell me what you put in there. You work on it awhile and I'll be right back." Patti left the room. Sharon sat motionless, staring into space. She wrote, dropped in a card and wrote again. Continuing to write, she reached for a tissue with her free hand. She wiped her nose and eyes. Finally, she sighed heavily, rested her head on the back of the couch, looking at the ceiling.

Presently, Patti returned. "All done?"

"I haven't decided what to do about Roger."

"What do you want to do?"

"He's such a good person and I feel so comfortable and safe when I'm with him..."

"Do you love him?"

"If I let myself, I could..."

"Lucky you, able to turn love on and off. Why don't you want to let yourself?"

"What if we got married and something happened to him? I don't want to be hurt."

"Who does? Do you have a guarantee that if you reject Roger and find someone else ... or live the rest of your life alone ... that you'll never be hurt?"

"Of course not."

"We're always exposed to pain as long as our lives connect with others. Only you can decide if what you might have with him is worth the risk. And..."

"What?"

"How would it be if you put his safety in the box? Nothing you can do about it but worry. Why not let God take care of it."

Sharon picked up a card and slowly began to write.

Chapter Thirty-Two

Sharon sat at the computer and clicked on the folder marked 'Roger.' He had written every week since Christmas. When she checked her email in early January, there were two messages waiting. She had toyed with the impulse to delete, but finally filed them away unread, adding to the folder each time another appeared.

Date: December 30, 2004
From: roger.johnson
To: sjordan

Hi Sharon: Want to tell you about Todd's Christmas program at school. He kept asking if I'd be there and seemed pretty excited about it. The big night came and Mom had him all dressed up. As it turned out, he spent the entire performance standing behind a piece of poster board that was decorated to look like a gift box. So much for my efforts with the video camera. After it was over the music teacher told me he volunteered – begged – for that part because he didn't want 'all those people looking at me.' I know he's a pretty shy little guy. Maybe one day he'll come out of his shell – er, box. As Ever, Roger

PS. I know I agreed to not talk about personal things but I have to say something: I hope and pray you will seek professional help to get over this trauma. That's all. I won't mention it again.

Date: January 6, 2005
From: roger.johnson
To: sjordan

I made a traffic stop last week and there was this pig sitting in the passenger seat. The lady said she had found the pig and didn't know what to do with it. I told her she should take him to the petting zoo. Today I stopped the same car and there was the pig, still there. I said, 'I thought I told you to take that pig to the zoo.' She said, 'I did and we had so much fun, now we're going to Disneyland.'

Okay, that didn't really happen – in fact it's a very old joke. But thought maybe you could use a smile today.

As always, Roger

Date: January 14, 2005
From: roger.johnson
To: sjordan

Hi Sharon: After last week you'll never believe me – but I swear this is true: Coming home tonight I was following this little Toyota and suddenly it starts swerving all over the road. Then she hits her brakes and pulls to the right and ends up with the front end in the ditch and the back wheels clear off the ground. When I got to the car and opened the door, a bird flew out in my face and I nearly had a heart attack. Seems this lady raises birds and she was making a delivery. She put the bird cage in the back seat next to her 3 year old in his car seat. While she was driving the little boy reached over and opened the cage. The bird flew out and went berserk there in the car. Luckily no one was hurt and when last seen the bird was in the top of a very tall tree. Hope you like this story. I may send it to Reader's Digest.

Always, Roger

Date: January 22, 2005
From: roger.johnson
To: sjordan

I know you've read about the tsunami that hit Asia about a month ago. With all the lives lost and devastation that is there, isn't it amazing how many stories of miracles we've heard? So much to wonder about when things like this happen. I am certainly not wise enough to offer any answers. But I was thinking today, it reminds me of something Paul (you know, in the Bible) said when he was in prison: Whether I live or whether I die, I am the Lord's. We don't know what the future holds but we know who's in charge and live or die, we belong to Him.   R.

Date: February 1, 2005
From: roger.johnson
To: sjordan

Today is my mom's birthday. She's 69. I haven't told you much about her, but you'd like her. After my dad died, 10 years ago, she surprised us all with her strength. He was the HEAD OF THE HOUSE (all capital letters!) – the decision maker. I wasn't sure Mom even knew how to write a check. But she showed us she could take care of things pretty well. She had never worked a day outside her home but she found a part time job and got active in the senior group at church. When Liz died, she stepped in, gave up her interests to take care of Todd. She's a wonderful person and I couldn't make it without her. I hope some day you two can meet. R.

Date: February 10, 2005
From: roger.johnson
To: sjordan

Sharon: It's really cold up here. Another big freeze. People bumping into each other and sliding all over the road – keeps me busy. Thank God no fatalities, but lots of bent fenders. The Weather Channel says Arkansas is cold and dry. Take care and stay warm. R.

Date: February 14, 2005
From: roger.johnson
To: sjordan

Today is Valentine's Day. Well, I'm not going to make the obvious statement. Afraid you don't want to hear it, if your silence is any indication. An exciting day for Todd. The rule in first grade is to bring a valentine for each member of the class. His teacher was kind enough to send home a list of kids and we spent last night writing names on the Spiderman cards he chose. Never thought of Spiderman as a messenger of love. But then, I'm not six years old.

Happy Valentine's Day. Roger

Date: February 22, 2005
From: roger.johnson
To: sjordan

I send these messages … like into a black hole. Not knowing how they are received, or even if they are read. It's lonely, this one-way communication. Well, it's not communication at all. Just me, writing words that may never be read. I wish the best for you, Sharon. And if I can't be a part of whatever that 'best' is, I guess I can deal with that. But could I just KNOW how you are? Are you happy? Hurting? Healing?

I've written words like this before only to delete them. This time I'll hit 'send.'
Roger

Sharon rose from the computer and, wrapping a coat around her, stepped onto the deck. With a flash of brilliant purple, a bird flitted from the wooden railing to the top of the bare maple tree. *Is that a Martin? Must be a scout. A sign that spring will surely come. Thank you, Lord, for the sign.* She shivered and drew herself deeper into the warmth of the coat. *Okay, Lord, here I am again. All my life I have heard stories about you. But I've always held you at arm's length. Now I want to know you personally … and your Son. I know it's time for me to stop living life vicariously on the faith of others. Reading the Bible to win a ribbon in Sunday School, being good to please my parents, attending church because it's important to Tim. This is me, Sharon, talking. I give you my life. I wrote it on the card and dropped it in the box. Now I beg you to send your Spirit to guide me and take care of me. Show me where I should go and I'll do my best to follow.*

Returning to the computer, Sharon blinked several times to clear her eyes before she clicked on the 'reply' icon.

Date: February 28, 2005

From: sjordan

To: roger.johnson

I'm healing. Just a little more time, please.

Sharon

Chapter Thirty-Three

Ohh... The dogwood is about to bloom. March definitely came in like a lamb. Sharon stopped the car in front of her house and picked up the mail. She scanned the envelopes, noting the information packet she had requested from Court Appointed Special Advocates, the organization for volunteers who work with children in foster care. The Habitat for Humanity logo on another envelope caught her attention. Her efforts to blitz the not-for-profit world with inquiries about employment or volunteerism were bringing results.

I'll run first, then look over all this after supper.

She hurried into the house, threw the mail on the kitchen counter and scooped up the ringing phone.

"Hello."

"Is this the Timothy Jordan residence?"

"Well … yes …"

"Am I speaking to Mrs. Jordan?"

"Yes …" She held her breath, overwhelmed at the déjà vu.

"This is Mike from Dish Network. How are you today?"

Sharon burst out laughing.

"Mrs. Jordan? Are you all right?"

"Oh, I'm sorry. I'm fine. But I don't need Dish. Thanks, anyway."

She hung up before Mike could protest, rushed to the office, flipped on the computer and waited impatiently for her email to open up. *It's been two weeks since we've written. It's time …*

Date: March 12, 2005

From: sjordan

To: roger.johnson

Dear Roger: One year ago today, you called to tell me my husband was dead. By the way, you were a little klutzy, did I ever tell you that? So much has happened this year, in many ways it seems longer than 365 days.

Sharon stopped typing. *How do I say this?*

I told my support group that I could not fathom finding someone to love the way I loved Tim. And I didn't. We love each person in our lives differently because the one who's loved brings unique qualities to the mix.

Boy, this is hard.

This past year, I've needed to find for myself who I am, who I'm supposed to be. Much of what has happened, and my handling of it – or my stumbling through it – has made me stronger. I know God is calling me to do something worthwhile with my life. But I have also come to believe that life will be better if you and I do it together.

Maybe as you read this you're thinking 'I told you so.' And you did. You seemed to know we should be together. And I think Eve and Patti knew. I guess I'm the last to know...

She stopped again, read over what she had written. *The heck with it.* She picked up the phone and rapidly punched the numbers.

"Johnson here."

The sound of his voice caused a tug on her heart. *Ah. I've missed you.*

"Hello, Roger. This is Sharon …"

Notes about the Author

Dorothy Hatfield was born in Texas, lived in Oklahoma and Tennessee and now makes her home in Arkansas. She is a free lance writer whose op-ed pieces have appeared in the Nashville Tennessean, the Arkansas Democrat Gazette and several regional newspapers. Her devotional material has been printed in The Upper Room, Mature Living, Evangel, Church Educator and Ministry Now. A collection of award-winning short stories was published in 2006 under the title *Every Day a New Day and other short stories.*

Dot is past president of White County Creative Writers and a founding member of Central Arkansas Writers. She encourages every serious writer to find a critique group or mentor.

The Last to Know is her first novel.

the last to know • dorothy hatfield

ne doorbell broke the silence of the house...

Sharon scrambled out of the recliner, tripping on the afghan draped over her legs. *Tim's home. He forgot his key.* She yanked open the door. The man on the stoop looked vaguely familiar.

"Mrs. Jordan?" He opened his hand to display an official looking badge. "I'm John Wilson from the Sherriff's Department. May I come in?"

Her heart tightened. *Something really has happened to Tim...*

from *The Last To Know*

Sharon Jordan is happily married and content with her life — until the afternoon she learns that her husband has been killed in a head-on collsion outside Lincoln, Nebraska. Sharon thought he was on a business trip to Dallas. Overwhelmed at her loss, she is determined to protect the memory of her husband. Her quest to peel away the layers of Tim's hidden life leads Sharon to a small town in Nebraska and back to the homeless shelters of Little Rock.

In *The Last To Know*, Dorothy Hatfield weaves a story of secrecy, grief, healing,and spiritual awakening.

ISBN 978-0-578-01728-0
90000
9 780578 017280

OTHATFIELD.COM

the last to know

A NOVEL

DOT HATFIELD

www.ingramcontent.com/pod-product-compliance
Lightning Source LLC
La Vergne TN
LVHW012332100826
845148LV00017B/2121

* 9 7 8 0 5 7 8 0 1 7 2 8 0 *